What's a
Black Critic
to Do?

What's a
Black Critic
to Do?

Interviews, Profiles and Reviews
of Black Writers

Donna Bailey Nurse

INSOMNIAC PRESS

National Library of Canada Cataloguing in Publication Data

Bailey Nurse, Donna, 1961-
        What's a black critic to do?: interviews, profiles and reviews of black writers / Donna Bailey Nurse.

ISBN 1-894663-52-7

1. Canadian literature (English)—Black-Canadian authors—History and criticism. 2. American literature—African American authors—History and criticism. 3. Race in literature. I. Title.

PS8089.5.B5B35 2003   C810.'896   C2003-904473-4

The publisher gratefully acknowledges the support of the Canada Council, the Ontario Arts Council and the Department of Canadian Heritage through the Book Publishing Industry Development Program. We acknowledge the support of the Government of Ontario through the Ontario Media Development Corporation's Ontario Book Initiative.

Printed and bound in Canada

Insomniac Press
192 Spadina Avenue, Suite 403
Toronto, Ontario, Canada, M5T 2C2
www.insomniacpress.com

THE CANADA COUNCIL | LE CONSEIL DES ARTS
FOR THE ARTS | DU CANADA
SINCE 1957 | DEPUIS 1957

ONTARIO ARTS COUNCIL
CONSEIL DES ARTS DE L'ONTARIO

For Jeff,
and for our children, Alex and Noelle

The English are so nice
so awfully nice
they're the nicest people in the world.

And what's more, they're nice about being nice
about your being nice as well!
If you're not nice, they soon make you feel it.

—D.H. Lawrence

I like talkin' about you you you you usually
But occasionally
I want to talk about me.

—Toby Keith

Table of Contents

Acknowledgements

Thanks to my editors at the *Globe and Mail*, *Maclean's*, the *Toronto Star* and the *Montreal Gazette*, who did not always grasp my perspective, but who encouraged me nonetheless, especially Bryan Demchinsky in Montreal and Dan Smith in Toronto. And many thanks, as well, to a very supportive friend, Elaine Kalman Naves, to my mother Sylvia Bailey for her generous encouragement, and to my husband Jefferson Nurse for his creative inspiration.

A number of the pieces in this book first appeared, often in a different form, in the *Montreal Gazette*, the *Globe and Mail*, the *National Post*, *Pride*, *Quill & Quire*, the *Toronto Star* and *Word*.

Preface

In the spring of 1999 I asked Noah Richler, my editor at the *National Post*, if he would be interested in my writing a column on black books from a black perspective. I told him I could call the column What's A Black Critic To Do?, which would be partly tongue-in-cheek. But Noah was not amused. "Donna," he responded tersely in his brisk British accent. "I did not hire you to be a black critic." He meant he hired me to be a critic with no colour attached. Naturally, this is a good thing.

Yet for me, the discussion is more complex than Richler would have it. The English language is the product of a white culture, and does not, as yet, fully embrace me. In English the word critic actually means "white critic," just as the word "woman" means "white woman." Whenever I show up to interview a writer, I can pretty much tell if they are expecting a critic instead of a black critic, a woman instead of a black woman. Those who are not expecting a black woman look mighty surprised to see me. This holds true whether the writer I am interviewing is black, white, or any other race.

The response does not bother me much, especially when it comes from white American authors. White American men, especially, are generally happy to see me, as are those from the international scene. The presence of a black female literary journalist suggests to them great social strides. Sometimes I can't even get these men to talk about their books. The late American critic Alfred Kazin said he never thought he'd see the day when he'd be interviewed by a woman like me, and he was glad, very glad, that things had come so far. The Irish-born Brian Moore wanted only to talk of race and Haiti. Mexico's Carlos Fuentes told me all about his favourite aunt, a mulatto, who was the product of a long-standing relationship between his grandfather and a black mistress. None of these kind men failed to notice that I am black. I'm okay with that because my race is an inextricable part of who I am. It is not all of who I am, but it is one important aspect.

And this is my approach to black writers: that race is an important aspect of who they are, and often an intrinsic element of their work. That is why I have devoted a good portion of my energies as a critic to studying what black writers choose to talk about, and how they choose to talk about it. I am interested in when the subject of race shows up and when it doesn't. I am interested in how black characters apprehend and navigate the world. I think black experience is as rich, diverse and compelling as white experience. I write to enlighten myself and other people of colour and white people as well, because we are all connected.

What's a Black Critic to Do? brings together profiles, reviews, interviews and essays primarily about black Canadian authors written over the last decade. Most of these pieces have appeared previously in newspapers and magazines, but a handful are published here for the first time. I have also included some writers of colour who are not black or West Indian—Ojibway writer Richard Wagamese and Indian-born writer Shauna Singh Baldwin are two—because I am curious about how other groups express their relationship to Canada and to the English language. A number of Americans who produce wonderful works about race and/or Caribbean experience, including novelists Toni Morrison, Edwidge Danticat and Jamaica Kincaid, and the documentary filmmaker, Ken Burns, have also been included.

My conclusions regarding black Canadian literature are really just beginning. I find, re-reading the pieces I've published over the years, that a few individual reviews do not reflect my overall sense of an author. My review of Cecil Foster's *Slammin' Tar* gave some readers the impression black Canadian literature can do without him. It can't. At the moment, my review of Dionne Brand's *At the Full and Change of the Moon* seems overly generous. Her poetry, however, especially *Land To Light On*, lingers deliciously in the mind.

Ultimately *What's a Black Critic to Do?* is for ordinary people who are looking for ways to talk about books and race, or movies and race, or theatre and race. Perhaps the book will help English teachers who are a little uneasy about the topic, or assist book club members in selecting a title. Hopefully the book will encourage journalists to think more critically about the work of black artists. If it accomplishes any of these goals, the effort has been worthwhile.

Donna Bailey Nurse
Market Street, Toronto, 2003

By Way of Introduction

The author Eudora Welty died this week. I'm sorry I never got to meet her. Welty's *One Writer's Beginnings* is one of the books I always keep close by. If I go out of town I pack it in with my necessities, alongside my toothbrush and towel. I've considered Welty a kind of a kindred spirit ever since I read these lines describing her earliest feelings about books:

> I cannot remember a time when I was not in love with them—the books themselves, cover and binding and the paper they were printed on, with their smell and their weight and their possession in my arms, captured and carried off to myself. Still illiterate, I was ready for them, committed to all the reading I could give them.

I never set out to be a critic, although now it seems like the only thing I was really ever meant to be. When packages of books appear at my door—as they do several times a week—it occasionally occurs to me that I've been opening my door to books for most of my life. It began with *Humpty Dumpty Magazine* which I'm pretty sure started showing up in the mail before I knew how to read. Soon I was receiving single books wrapped in brown paper. American series like the Bobbsey Twins and The Happy Hollisters; Trixie Beldon and, of course, Nancy Drew.

I figured out pretty soon that people presumed bookish children were intelligent, which in my case was a good thing, considering the competition. My little sister was cute as a button, smiley and sweet. She had our relatives eating out of her hands.

"Well Donna is the *reader*!" my mother would say, and my relatives would nod their approval. My sister was not only a beautiful child, she could sing, dance and act. Whenever I complained about my lack of a special talent, my mother would say, "Well somebody has to be in the audience. You make a *great* audience Donna!"

So I became a critic.

I don't mean to imply that I turned to writing about books by default. Because that's not true at all. If I think about it I was analyzing literature for a long while.

I grew up in Pickering, Ontario, and from the time I was about seven or eight I attended the Presbyterian Church in Pickering Village. In my teens we had a youth group in which the Bible was studied. Among other things, the Bible is a giant book of stories. During a Bible study we would talk about plot and character and metaphor and theme. Of course, if you asked us we would have said we were simply trying to discover the meaning we were meant to take from a psalm, parable or verse. But that is exactly what criticism is about—the extraction of meaning.

I had no idea what I wanted to do when I got to university. I was lost. But I gravitated toward English literature. During high school I had had casual, superficial encounters with books. Outside of *The Hobbit* I can hardly remember what I studied. It was in university that literature was reborn for me. It was like being a child again.

One university course in particular had an impact. That was Russell Brown's class on the short story. It's where I had my first serious interaction with Alice Munro, Mavis Gallant and Margaret Laurence. Especially Laurence's *A Bird in the House*. For me, *A Bird in the House* is like Welty's *One Writer's Beginnings*. I don't leave town without it.

But the prose I admire most is probably Mavis Gallant's. My own copy of her *Paris Notebooks*, which contains her writings about Paris in the '60s, is so bedraggled that lately I've taken to borrowing a copy from the library. I have never actually got around to reading the notebook entries about the Paris student demonstrations. What I like about *Paris Notebooks* are the essays and reviews, the pieces on the Anglo-Irish writer Elizabeth Bowen and Colette and Marguerite Yourcenar, writers I know next to nothing about, but who come alive to me through Gallant's stylish prose. I reread a review of hers at least once a week.

I also read and reread her short stories, many of which are set in Paris just after the war. A favourite story of mine is "The Picnic," in which an American officer stationed outside Paris is responsible for putting together a small community picnic. Officer Marshall and his wife are feeling stressful about the occasion. The story opens like this: "The three Marshall children were up and dressed for the picnic before their father was awake. Their mother had been up since dawn, for the coming day of pleasure weighed heavily on her mind."

Every time I read "the coming day of pleasure weighed heavily on her mind" I feel like laughing. What a perfect way to describe the oppressive glee of holidays.

At university, I was also introduced to the Victorian novel. I still consider Elizabeth Gaskell and George Eliot among my favourite authors and probably among my favourite people. We think we are so far gone from the Victorian age, but I think it is still with us, especially in the expectations ordinary women have for their family lives. The cult of domesticity thrives. But Victorian heroines also struggle with their desire to make their own way in the world, financially and intellectually, and to locate an enduring love. Some very popular contemporary writers are actually Victorian writers: the American Anita Shreve, a number of Indo-Canadian writers, Anita Rau Badami and I think Shyam Selvadurai, also some black women writers like Jamaica Kincaid. Jamaica Kincaid's heroines, like Victorian heroines, lack the guidance and comfort of a mother's love.

At university I studied the history of criticism with Patricia Vicari. I took it twice actually. The first time I dropped out. I liked studying the Victorian critics like Matthew Arnold and Henry James, and the modern critics like I.A. Richards. But I was daunted by the idea of the early critics, Aristotle and Plato, and especially Longinus and Horace. I tried the course again when I returned to school in the early '90s to extend my three-year degree to four. And much to my surprise these writers began to make sense to me.

I don't remember much of the course now, but sometimes while I'm reading a book or writing a review some little thing will occur to me and I will go and find my course text, *The Great Critics: An Anthology of Literary Criticism*, and scavenge about in there until I uncover what I'm looking for. The criticism course was invaluable in terms of understanding books. It confirmed for me the lasting importance of both stories and criticism. These days, you hear a lot of griping about critics, as though we are an alien species, a plague upon writers from another planet. The truth is that critics have been critiquing stories just about as long as storytellers have been telling them.

I always loved reading popular criticism. By the time I was a teenager I was reading more book reviews than books. I liked the way critics talked about plots and characters as though they were actual and significant and not abstractions. I also liked reading the introductions to books, which a lot of people skip over.

Characters in books are often more real to me than people. I can generally determine what makes a character tick. Real people are a good deal harder to figure out.

I started writing seriously with a review in the *Toronto Star*. I was home with my second child who was a few months old. Before that I had published a couple of pieces in the black newspapers *Share* and *Contrast*. I sent Judy Stoffman, who was then Books Editor at the *Star*, a few of these published articles and a note asking her if she would be interested in assigning me a book to review.

Then I forgot about it. About three weeks later I received a package with a book called *Frontiers*, a collection of essays by the black Canadian writer M. Nourbese Philip. There was a note attached. It read:

Dear Donna,

Here is a book for review as you requested. Your deadline is two weeks. The fee will be $150. I could not get in touch with you by phone. If you are serious about freelancing you will need to get an answering machine.

Sincerely,
Judy Stoffman.

I always think how lucky I was that Judy didn't simply give up when she couldn't contact me by phone. That was the first lesson I learned about the business. Be easily accessible. If the editor can't reach you, you won't get the job.

Each editor has taught me something new. At *Maclean's* I learned to get used to rejection. I sent them thirteen proposals. They assigned me one book. From that time I understood that I better get used to hearing the word "No." When you send in thirteen proposals and only one is accepted, you know that that one better be good. So I stopped worrying about quantity and started focusing on quality. I thought if each piece could be as strong as possible the assignments would follow and for the most part this has been true.

I think I learned my most important lesson at the *Globe and Mail*. I had approached the entertainment editor James Adams with a story about black Canadian art. He accepted the idea but he wasn't happy with the result. It was a fairly large piece and he felt I had written it too much in the style of an essay. "But take it back and work on it some more," he said. "I think you can do it."

I listened to his criticisms and reworked the piece. I handed it back to him a few days later. "This is good," he said, "This is just what I wanted." James taught me that I could fail and then fix it. And this has been a great lesson, not just for writing, but for life.

I also learned from James how to accept criticism. Because you have to be able to take your editor's advice. And if you think about it, getting advice from some of the greatest editors in the country is a bonus. It is one of the best and easiest ways of honing your craft. I can never understand writers who continuously resist criticism from their editors.

Still, I do think you have to be able to trust that editor's integrity and intelligence. I have had tremendous good fortune in this regard. Sometimes junior editors can lack subtlety and sensitivity, but the senior editors I've worked for have been a font of knowledge and a source of encouragement.

I write mostly about books and authors, but not solely. Sometimes I write about theatre, television or music. And frequently I incorporate the subject of race. Race is a difficult topic to write about in Canada, because people find it offensive. In addition, a woman who talks about race—even a black woman—is considered grossly unladylike.

I continue to do it because I feel a sense of responsibility, especially to my children. People ask me if I am a writer or a black writer. Well I'm a black woman writer. If race makes its way into a discussion, this is the position I take. For one thing, I want to make sure black women have a chance of having their views heard. Of course, my views will not coincide with the position of every black woman. But there is a good chance I will share the views of many. Besides, the voice of a sole black woman is as important as anyone else's voice. It deserves to be heard.

Last December I wrote a piece in the *National Post* about black women and their church hats. Ellen Vanstone, the editor, did a fabulous job displaying the black-and-white photos of several black American women in dramatic hats. I got excited just thinking about a black woman coming upon the paper and finding someone like herself elegantly depicted. That piece meant a great deal to me.

One of the main concerns I have about race is that often two separate discussions are taking place, by which I mean black people often say different things privately amongst themselves, than they do in public. This is only natural. When I interview a black artist, if it is appropriate, I try to encourage the kind of conversation that will make white people privy to what we really feel. In other words, I don't want there to always be two separate discussions taking place. I don't think that's helpful.

When I write reviews I feel like I'm having a conversation with the writer. I am responding to his or her ideas, his or her perspectives. Of course I would much rather speak with them in person, which is the main reason I enjoy writing feature profiles. It's an opportunity to spend time with interesting people. I can't think of another profession in which I would be invited to spend the day with Toni Morrison or an hour in dialogue with Carlos Fuentes or breakfast with Jamaica Kincaid. In what other career would I find myself having coffee with Angela Davis, the courageous black advocate of the '70s? In what other life would I be able to hear Angela Davis—my hero from the age of 14—call *me* brave? These are the perks of my job, and they are considerable.

The conversation I most enjoy is the one I have with my readers. I just love knowing that through a review or an article I may be talking to hundreds of people, that the review may move them to purchase the book, or if they don't actually purchase the book, they might be interested enough in something I've said, perhaps about race, to think about an issue differently. Maybe someone out there will feel more supported. All of this is possible to achieve through writing. I would like to write regularly for magazines, because they pay more money. But I love the idea of writing the best pieces I can for a newspaper audience, and knowing that if I do it well, someone will be entertained and enlightened for a mere fifty cents. I think that's a bargain. [Humber School of Creative Writing, Summer 2001]

Profiles

After the Giller

Austin Clarke sweeps through the atrium of the Grand Hotel in downtown Toronto. The wool overcoat cast loosely over his shoulders billows out behind him like a cape. It is 6:15 and he is late. In the bar, the formally attired staff flock about him like friendly penguins. "Good evening Mr. Clarke." "This table Mr. Clarke?" "Your usual?" A dry martini materializes before him. He takes a sip and sinks with a pleasant sigh into the wingback chair.

Since last November, when Clarke, 68, won the Giller Prize for *The Polished Hoe*, he has been in great demand. He has just come from the photographer's studio, he explains. Earlier he was the guest of the seniors' class at George Brown College that is studying his work:"Very flattering." Afterward, he was taken to lunch at the college's cooking school: "It was delicious," says Clarke, himself an accomplished cook. A few weeks ago he visited Trinidad, Jamaica, and his native Barbados for the Caribbean launch of his book. In June, Clarke will deliver a keynote address at Book Expo Canada in Toronto.

For dinner we are seated on the terrace, which, in late March, is closed in and heated. The room is dim and strung with white lights. Out of the quiet, a feminine cry: "Austin! Is that you?" A tall, blond woman scurries over. "My neighbour," Clarke says, making introductions. The woman hovers solicitously: "Now, don't forget, Austin. You are coming with us this weekend. You will travel in our car." She smiles brightly before reluctantly turning away.

The waitress serves a dish made specially for Clarke: Pasta and shrimp, sautéed in garlic and olive oil, and garnished with parsley, a sprinkling of parmesan cheese. There is plenty, so we share. We drink Amarone from goblets as deep as bowls. "Cheers," says Austin Clarke, lifting his glass.

Winning the Giller Prize, Canada's top prize for fiction, has transformed Clarke into a bona fide literary star, though he claims not to be fascinated by celebrity: "I am aware of all the flattering appendages that go along with celebrity and I sometimes wallow in them, and sometimes take them with a grain of salt," he says.

He is waxing philosophical, but anyone can see how happy he is, how thrilled he continues to be. He received word of another boost in early March when *The Polished Hoe* won the regional Commonwealth Writers Prize for best book in Canada and the Caribbean.

The novel is set in the 1950s on the West Indian island of Bimshire (a fictionalized version of Barbados), where Mary Mathilda, the privileged black mistress of a cruel plantation manager confesses to a brutal crime. The plot consists of the long involved statement given by Mary to the police officer. The novel delves into Mary's past and into the dark history of racial oppression on the island and around the world.

Clarke has been plugging away, valiantly, for nearly forty years. This is his tenth novel. He has six collections of short stories. In 1997, his novel *The Origin of Waves* won the Rogers Writers' Trust Fiction Prize. All of his books examine, with pathos and humour, the condition of the West Indian at home and in Canada. Tonight he makes the most un-Canadian of admissions: he feels his success is deserved.

"For many years I wondered why my work had received such scant attention," he says. "Not only because I imagined the literary quality of my books, but because I was aware of the amount of work I had put into my writing."

For Clarke, the most important thing about the Giller is the critical acknowledgement it bestows: "I would be a fool to say that the Giller is meaningless," he says. "It is important insofar as legitimacy might be given to ideas which I have been talking about for years."

In structure, *The Polished Hoe* shares the jazzy modernity of African-American novels like *The Cattle Killing* by John Edgar Wideman, *Song of Solomon* by Toni Morrison and the young upstart, Colson Whitehead's *John Henry Days*. Clarke reproduces a vernacular, replete with calypsos and singing games, that shapes and embodies black experience. Many of the reviews that greeted the novel were exuberant. In the *Toronto Star*, critic Shaun Smith described the book as an unqualified masterpiece, "a novel of Biblical proportions and Homeric grandeur." Tim McNamara in the *Edmonton Journal* compared the work to Faulkner. Even writers who expressed reservations about the book's improvisational style—T.F. Rigelhof, for instance, in the *Globe and Mail*—heralded *The Polished Hoe* as a major accomplishment.

But a funny thing happened on the way to the Giller. The morning of the ceremony the *Globe and Mail* held a mock jury, praising Clarke's use of the vernacular, but panning what they described as the book's shapelessness. In the jury's opinion, a win for Clarke was a long shot. It was what occurred after his Giller win, however, that gave Clarke pause. A number of influential critics went on record naming Guy Vanderhaege's novel *The Last Crossing* as the best book of the year. Vanderhaege had been left off the shortlists of both the Giller Prize and the Governor General's Awards, and many critics had expressed their consternation. Still, the near unison of these remarks, in the first flush of Clarke's Giller win, felt like a public slap. What bothered Clarke, most of all, were implications in some literary circles that he had won because he was black. He felt there were those out to demean his accomplishment by turning it into an act of affirmative action. Clarke was "annoyed and depressed."

"I was disappointed by some of the remarks made by some of the so-called literary gurus of this city and country...I felt their comments were bordering on an unspeakable attitude. It was alarming. But then, of course, it was not alarming, because I have lived here too long to be alarmed," says Clarke.

"The point, is if these critics are unwilling to accept the verdict of the first jury (for the Giller Prize), are they then willing accept the verdict of the second?" He is referring, of course, to his Commonwealth win.

These are fighting words from a man whom we are accustomed to viewing as part of the literary establishment. Certainly, there is no other black Canadian author who has been so heartily embraced as Austin Clarke—not the amiable George Elliott Clarke, not the bewitching Dionne Brand, not even the erudite Andre Alexis. But tonight I am hearing echoes of an earlier Clarke, the "rabble-rouser"(his words) of the 1960s and '70s, whom the *Toronto Star* once described as the angriest black man in Canada. He was a figure of his times, a product of the independence movements sweeping Africa and the Caribbean. He was stirred by the civil rights revolution to the south where he went for a while to teach at Duke and Yale. He wrote stinging articles indicting racism in Toronto. He was managing editor of *Contrast*, the outspoken organ of the Toronto's black community. He struggled against apartheid, picketing city stores that sold South African goods. His volatility extended to his early career. He thought publishers "a damn lot of fools," and was not afraid to say so.

Clarke has mellowed with age. But the embers of the hot young rebel smoulder still: "I have felt for a long time," says Clarke, "that there was a reservation so far as what I would call the natural acceptance of literature that could not be determined to be Canadian, although naturally nowadays, it is Canadian. How do you define a Canadian writer? Is a Canadian writer a person who is born here, and whose family goes back two or three generations, and whose sensibilities are so Canadian that he has got to write about Canadians? And if he writes about Canadians, are we subliminally saying that his characters have got to be white?

"*The Polished Hoe* is a Canadian novel," he continues. "It is not a book about Barbados, so much as it is a book about people in this country who are from Barbados and who are reflecting back two or three generations. It is true we don't have sugar cane plantations or slave plantations today in Canada. But when slavery was raging throughout the world, it was not absent from the Canadian psyche."

We are finishing up our meal, savouring the last of the wine. We agree to pursue the conversation tomorrow afternoon at his home around the corner. Clarke wonders if perhaps he has said too much. But the next day he is even more vociferous.

"How about [Rohinton] Mistry?" Clarke demands. We are sitting in his office on the second floor. Pale gold sunlight is filtering through a window overlooking the street. "There is an argument," he says, "that Mistry is not a Canadian author because his books are not set in Canada. But Mistry could in fact be writing about members of the South Asian population who are scattered throughout this country in significant numbers. And not only in significant numbers, but in politically significant numbers. They are premiers. They are ministers in government.

"I'm saying you could walk along Parliament near Bloor," he adds, "walk along some street in Mississauga—you could go out in Vancouver—and see the people represented in Mistry's prose. And these people are only one step removed from the continent." It is precisely because Mistry has absorbed the ethos of the multicultural Canadian society, insists Clarke, that makes him a Canadian writer.

Today Clarke is wearing a navy tracksuit with the letters J-A-M-A-I-C-A stitched in large letters across the back. He ran track in his youth and his movements remain light and agile. He bounds out to the kitchen, brings me tea in a bone china cup. He rests it on the pages of the Bible lying open on his desk. There is nowhere else to put it. Every horizontal surface is piled with reading material or rows of photographs. There is absolutely no bare wall in the living room or office—where bookshelves leave off, framed paintings, posters and clippings begin. Everyone Clarke has ever loved or admired is represented here, as is his every achievement. There are pictures of his three daughters and Betty his ex-wife, and his mother who is in her late 80s and resides in the US. I see Norman Mailer, Miles Davis, Malcolm X, C.L.R. James, The Honourable Barbara McDougall. There is the glorious cover from *The Polished Hoe*, and over his desk, the *Globe*'s splendid caricature of the Giller nominees. The atmosphere is saturated in meaning. Clarke is surrounded by all of his life.

Clarke cannot offer me food, for, as usual, he has little on hand. Though he loves to cook, it is rare that he eats more than one meal per day. Earlier this afternoon an appreciative student took Clarke out for lunch—he will not eat again until tomorrow, or the day after. He began fasting regularly in the 1960s on the advice of a friend, Malcolm X.

Students play a significant role in Clarke's life. They are forever calling up for encouragement, treating him to thank-you dinners. He has just wrapped up a stint as Writer in Residence at the Toronto Reference Library where he helped would-be writers polish their manuscripts. He is the inspiration behind *McGill Street*, a journal founded several years ago by a group of Humber College students who met regularly at his

McGill Street home. More recently, he helped establish *Pagitica* with former members of his summer writing class from the Taddle Creek workshop at the University of Toronto. In 1999 Clarke was awarded the W.O. Mitchell Prize in recognition of his extensive body of work and his commitment to young writers.

Since winning the Giller, however, Clarke has not had a moment to commit to his own writing. Put plainly, he has rarely picked up a pen. He is hoping to resume work on a second memoir that starts off where the first, *Growing Up Stupid Under the Union Jack*, concluded. It will begin with Clarke's arrival at Trinity College in Canada in 1955, and follow his life through to the present day. He has also been working on a novel called *More*, which he abandoned in the 1970s. He got a good start on it last autumn, but then he won the Giller Prize.

Clarke also has a collection of selected stories due out in the fall called *Choosing His Coffin*. The title entry is one of a handful of new pieces included in the book. It is a humorous, fictionalized account of a trip he made to New Jersey to help his mother purchase a burial plot for her dying husband (Clarke's stepfather). In the story, the mother's anxiety about mortality makes her susceptible to fainting spells. But Clarke harbours no such fears: "I have never put too much stress on the consideration of my mortality," he says. "I'm more disposed to consider my immortality. My mortality will take care of itself and of me.

"But if I had a way of handling my immortality, I would lay down the foundation to make sure I would be remembered. Many times I have considered writing my own obituary, but only a revisionist version."

Clarke has no plans to retire. He feels he has at least four big novels left in him. He would also like to experiment with a book of longer stories. Besides, why should he slow down now? His Giller win promises increased critical interest, wider audiences, and, after forty long years, decent advances: "Let's just say," says Clarke, "that the Giller and its name cannot be underestimated. Whereas I am not disposed to alerting either creditors or income tax agents as to my predisposition to settle accounts, I can say that one consequence of having won the Giller is a refreshing monetary re-evaluation of my work."

The other consequence is Clarke's heightened celebrity, which carries with it the pleasure of being recognized and therefore welcomed wherever he goes. This is important, says Clarke, because a writer needs to get out.

"Being a writer restricts you into a room and that can be very depressing—it usually is depressing—and you need some release from that environment.

"And what better release," says Clarke, "than to come out of your cocoon and see real people. And then, of course, in the act of seeing these real people, and interacting with these real people, is the determination to go back into your little corner and create." [*Quill&Quire*, 2003]

Roots Canadian Style

Why we always makin' God feel
Downright broken, pissed off, an' tired
With our sorry assed, po-mouthed prayers?
If prayer could bust iron, we'd be free.

—from *Beatrice Chancy* (1999)

Nova Scotia poet George Elliott Clarke is one of the few African-Canadians who can trace both sides of his family all the way back to slavery. "My mother's family were slaves in the area around Chesapeake Bay," says Clarke. "They were liberated by the British during the War of 1812 and settled in Liverpool, Nova Scotia. My father's side is descended from a slave in Kings County, Virginia—a carpenter who was allowed to purchase his freedom. My father's maternal grandfather, William Andrew White, arrived from Virginia in the late 1890s to attend Acadia University."

For Clarke, then, slaves are not abstract historical figures, but his own beloved relations. Clarke's recently published verse play, *Beatrice Chancy*, is based on his opera about slavery in Canada. The story oozes with a sense of familial affection. It is safe to say that Clarke embraces a slave history many of us would just as soon forget. Clarke remains unequivocal about his roots: "You have to accept where you come from, no matter what it is. I can't deny my past, and there's no reason why I should."

Clarke called me recently from North Carolina where he has spent the last several years teaching Canadian literature at Duke University. He spoke in an eager, earnest and slightly breathless manner that made him sound considerably younger than his nearly forty years. Our conversation was hurried as he was off to Vienna shortly where he was scheduled to attend a conference on multiculturalism in the arts.

From Vienna he travelled to Toronto, arriving just in time for the opening of *Beatrice Chancy* at Harbourfront's du Maurier Theatre. The opera is a collaboration between Clarke and Canadian composer James Rolfe. It tells the story of a young mulatto woman, the child of a dissolute white master and his slave mistress. Master Chancy adores his beautiful daughter, but his love turns to rage when she professes her desire for a slave.

Clarke's libretto blends the music of the King James Bible with the moodiest blues, romantic poetry and Elizabethan drama. He has used some of the loftiest British traditions to immortalize the slave experience: "I don't apologize for using Elizabethan language in a work about Canadian slavery," Clarke said. "I see the flavour as absolutely appropriate. I felt compelled to go there. I am answering back to Shakespeare and to Dante and to Shelley."

Add *Beatrice Chancy* to Clarke's oeuvre celebrating the timbre and the texture of Black Nova Scotia, a culture Clarke himself has labelled Africadian. Clarke has edited an anthology of Black Nova Scotian writing, as well as a collection of African-Canadian works called *Eyeing the North Star* (1997). His books of poetry include *Saltwater Spirituals and Deeper Blues* (1983), *Lush Dreams, Blue Exile* (1994), and best of all, *Whylah Falls* (1990).

In *Whylah Falls*, Clarke relies upon a pastiche of forms—sketches, verse, prose and photographs—to limn the lives of Blacks in a mythic, rural Nova Scotian town in the 1930s. Here is an excerpt from a world he describes as a "northern Mississippi":

> The Jarvis County moon has turned up as gold as
> Selah's Selassian vision of Africa. Pleased, Selah
> reclines, making soap go crazy in the tub. She
> thinks luxury is what the twenties were about and
> she don't care who disagrees. Later, extracted and
> rubbed down she moans into her diary, 'I'll never
> be, I'll never be, I'll never be married.' She
> dreams herself laced lusciously in white, her dark
> breasts coddled by white silk as if they were
> delicately wrapped bonbons or two verses from The
> Song of Solomon.

George Elliott Clarke was born in Windsor Plains, Nova Scotia, in 1960, the first of three boys belonging to William and Geraldine Clarke. The family soon settled in Halifax's north end. Clarke's mother taught school in North Preston, in a provincial education system that remained largely segregated. Clarke's father worked for CN. In those days a job with the railway was just about the most secure and lucrative position a black man could have, and this afforded the family a comfortable, middle-class existence.

"My father was a baggage handler who slowly moved up the ranks to ticket agent," Clarke recalled. "But in his private time he was strongly oriented toward the arts. When he was young he even performed at the Neptune Theatre.

"My father worked nights and was home during the day and I remember he would listen to classical music on his Clairtone stereo. The stereo was produced locally and it had a unique and beautiful sound. And I remember that when I did my homework, Dad's music—Strauss waltzes, like the "Blue Danube," and the songs of the Peruvian singer Yma Sumac—would be playing in the background.

"My mother on the other hand, was much more at home with black music, with soul and with rhythm and blues. She loved her Wilson Pickett and she loved her James Brown."

Clarke's parents divorced when he was 14 years old. But he received plenty of family support from his maternal grandparents who lived in rural Hants County. Clarke and his brother would visit them on weekends. The boys stayed with their grandparents for entire weeks at a time during summer vacation, and it was here Clarke first encountered Nova Scotia's black folk culture: "In Hants County all the entertainment in the world took place at home. On a Friday night people would sit down to a meal of fried smelt or crispy trout with vinegar and salt. After dinner they would have a couple of beers and people would always drop by. They'd dance to music on the record player—some country and western and some rhythm and blues. Then about 11 o'clock or so, someone would start singing a cappella. Someone else would join in and then somebody would go get their guitar or their fiddle. My great uncle Charlie made a living fiddling all across the Annapolis Valley."

Clarke speaks warmly of a black Canadian presence that is more than two hundred years old. He writes poems meant to etch that culture into the landscape of our minds. Above all his poetry thrums with admiration for a race of survivors: "Slavery took away our language; took away our religion. They said 'Don't play your music!' But somehow black people managed to retain much of the power of their original culture. You simply can't crush everything out of a people. And I think that is something to celebrate." [*Pride*, 1999]

Two Solitudes

Jamaican author Olive Senior peoples her latest collection of stories, *Discerner of Hearts* (1995), with pleasingly familiar characters. Old women, like the widowed Miss Evadney in the story "The Chocho Vine," exist in practically every Jamaican village. Miss Evadney describes her varied infirmities to anyone who will listen. "Ai my dear, the gas, the gas da kill me," and "She would commence rubbing that part of her anatomy which was currently the locus of her pain. . . ."

The stern but loving family helper also appears regularly in Senior's tales. Country women like Desrine, in "Zig Zag," who relies on a local healer—as well as protein—to ensure her eldest daughter's academic success. "Is not little bush Miss Mary use on that Manuela there... Plenty candle burn. Plenty fish head boil even when them other one don't get, for them don't need brain food yet." Senior's impeccably recorded dialect animates the most incidental characters.

Even before it became fashionable to do so, Senior insisted upon her characters speaking in the vernacular. For Senior, who avoids grand gestures, the decision was not political. "I just saw it as a part of the 'true to life' reality that I was describing." Today such bold use of the vernacular seems visionary. In 1987 Senior was recognized with a Commonwealth Writer's Prize for her first collection, *Summer Lightning* (1986). But, in the 1960s, when Senior first began churning out stories, native dialect was an accuracy few writers could afford to embrace. The desire to raise patois to literary status was an ill-received concept, particularly among educated Jamaicans of Senior's generation, who came of age before the island's independence from Britain in 1962. The handful of authors brave enough to reproduce Creole relied upon a sort of bastardized language that satisfied metropolitan standards, something Senior refused to do. As a result it took years for publishers to seriously consider her work.

Senior grew up during the colonial period, when English was not merely the norm, but the only language acceptable for learning. Senior describes the Montego Bay school she attended as a child: "You couldn't speak patois, you had to speak English. We were being socialized to become little English men and women."

In the Trelawny village where Senior was born the Jamaican language prevailed alongside enduring African traditions. Villagers visited herb doctors and spiritual leaders practiced *obeah* and wore *guzus* to protect themselves from *duppy*. In the evenings the little girl would listen to stories about Anansi.

While the village did maintain a social hierarchy of sorts, says Senior, "Everyone was equal in a way. All of us played together. It didn't matter if you wore shoes or if you were barefoot. I was taught to respect all people, especially adults."

Around the age of eight, Senior left Trelawny to live with her mother's prosperous relatives in Westmoreland: "My adoptive family was close to white. And I was very conscious that we were the property owners and that I was expected to behave in a certain way. I couldn't go out and play with those barefoot kids again."

Senior travelled back and forth between the village and her new home in Westmoreland, oscillating between two different cultures and two separate set of values. She lived a double life. Even as a child she understood that her educated peers and relatives would scorn her village traditions. "You couldn't admit that you knew anything about the other life; that African world."

Senior claims that the rural village has enriched her most. She attempts to reclaim its African customs through her stories and poems, including the collection *Gardening in the Tropics* (1994), as well as through her scholarly work. She is also compiling an encyclopedia of Jamaican folklore.

Senior's use of dialect celebrates the non-colonial aspects of Jamaican culture. She releases patois from its subordinate role: "The margin is penetrating the centre. English literature is no longer looking to England. There's a sort of internationalization of literature. And that's good. Because we cannot say English is correct and everything else is bad."

Senior considers herself bilingual. She wants her writing to reflect both British literary and African oral storytelling traditions: "I have not one, but two, influences on my work," she says, "and I think for a writer that's a wonderful opportunity." [*Metro Word*, 1995]

Figure in a Landscape

A ndre Alexis was just four years old when he arrived in Canada from Trinidad. "I still have the memory of the first time I saw snow and how odd Canada was in terms of everything I knew about the world."

His confusion was compounded when his parents sent him to a French language school. "I was potentially French and potentially Canadian while at the same time feeling anglophone and Trinidadian. Having to find some sort of contact between these states has made me absolutely attentive to the little details of Canadian language, to the way the land looks and the way the land smells."

The attentiveness has brought rewards. The author's evocation of the Canadian landscape, and his characters' relationship with it, is as true and certain as anything in Margaret Laurence or Alice Munro. The particular originality that distinguishes his work stems from his own quest for belonging in the Canadian hinterland.

Alexis's play *Lambton Kent* has been revised to open the 1999 International Festival of Authors. Gutter Press is simultaneously publishing the text for the first time. Though neither publisher nor writer seem to have given the play much thought since it first appeared in 1995, its re-emergence could add momentum to the wave of public interest following the success of Alexis' first novel, *Childhood* (1998).

The play unfolds in the form of a lecture given by a renowned Nigerian anthropologist, Dr. K. Mtubu, who recounts the bizarre folk rituals he encounters on his travels through southern Ontario. It is a mischievous, satirical, at times patently absurd take on European studies of African cultures. But it is also the chronicle of an outsider who attempts to excavate meaning from a foreign landscape.

Greg Gatenby, artistic director of the International Festival of Authors, describes *Lambton Kent* as a small gem. "It's like finding an early work of Timothy Findley's or Margaret Atwood's."

This year Alexis shared Ontario's highest literary honour, the Trillium Award, for *Childhood*. With the success of his first novel, Alexis feels he can finally call himself a writer, a title he avoided laying claim to even after the positive reception of his collection *Despair: And Other Stories of Ottawa* in 1994. "With *Despair*, I was just learning to dream on paper," Alexis told me in 1998. "The process of writing the stories was the process of learning to trust the internal mechanism."

Likewise, he feels light years removed from the young author who penned *Lambton Kent*. He admits he had a hard time readying the play for the festival.

"It was difficult," he explains, "because I was revising the work of a novice writer. I've changed so much. I didn't want to screw up my own work, in the sense of making it better, according to who I am now. It was difficult to have respect for myself and yet respect for the past. It was very odd."

Nevertheless, he is excited about the new production, especially because the part of Professor Mtubu will be played by female actor Yanna McIntosh. Says Alexis, "Most of my work is destined for a woman, for my mother or my daughter or my sisters. A woman on stage reading my work feels entirely appropriate."

Alexis was born in Trinidad in 1957 and moved to Canada in 1961. He grew up in Ottawa and attended Carleton University where he studied Russian and philosophy and devoured a wide array of literature. He developed a particular admiration for Irish playwright Samuel Beckett for his use of distance and irony. Alexis worked as a bookseller for fifteen years, and when he embarked upon a literary career in the early 1990s he decided to write plays as well as short stories.

"Beckett wrote plays and that made it seem a legitimate thing for a writer to do."

In person, Alexis recalls an older generation of writers. Although he looks as though he is in his early 30s, he lacks the determined hipness that marks so many of his contemporaries. He smokes—a lot—and dresses with rumpled nonchalance. His references are broad, cosmopolitan, largely European. His conversation possesses a vaguely Edwardian sense of decorum.

His voice, a tender, sandy growl, takes one aback. It contributed greatly to the effect when, in 1994, he read from *Despair: And Other Stories of Ottawa* at the Rivoli on Queen Street West in Toronto. The book, in which the nation's sedate capital is depicted as deliciously macabre, was given an unmistakably gothic air.

Many of the scenes in *Lambton Kent* share a gothic flavour. Professor Mtubu is bemused by the inhabitants' ritualistic preoccupation with sweater-eating moths, cow skulls, bibles and dead bodies. Indeed, Alexis' work seems to contain elements of a genre increasingly recognized as southern Ontario gothic, as noted in the work of Raymond Knister, Alice Munro, Margaret Atwood and others.

But Alexis rejects the label: "My work is not gothic because I'm not really interested in darkness. I am more concerned with questions like 'How do we face death?' or 'Does God Exist?'

"In *Lambton Kent*, professor Mtubu is in a frustrating situation because as she travels through southern Ontario she finds the apparatus she brought with her for her anthropological studies inappropriate for the strange behaviours she encounters. Finally, she just gives up and begins to get in touch with what is essential everywhere, which is people, place, death, life."

Alexis' work exhibits an intimate engagement with the Canadian landscape, a propensity rare among immigrant authors and even rarer among Canadians of African descent. But it is precisely his immigrant sensibility that causes him to embrace the land as he does. [*National Post*, 1999]

An Optimistic Planet

One reason Canadian filmmaker Clement Virgo agreed to make *The Planet of Junior Brown* (1997) into a movie was because the book reminded him of Charles Dickens.

"I just love Dickens," says Virgo.

Dickens? The creator of such films as *A Small Dick Fleshy Ass Thang* (1991), *Save My Lost Nigga' Soul* (1993) and *Rude* (1995) loves Dickens?

"Oh, yeah! Dickens. Absolutely," nods Virgo, who lists *Great Expectations* among his favourite novels. "More than a hundred years ago Dickens was writing about child labour and poverty and street kids. Today you can't walk half a block without a homeless kid begging you for money. *The Planet of Junior Brown* allowed me to make some direct parallels between what was happening in nineteenth-century London and what is happening at the end of the twentieth century in North America."

Virgo first grabbed the attention of Canadian audiences with his 1995 feature *Rude*. The film boldly linked the stories of three different characters—a drug dealer who has just been released from prison, a boxer who is a closet homosexual, and a woman who has lost her boyfriend after having an abortion. The movie won a jury citation at the Toronto International Film Festival and received international kudos after playing at the film festival in Cannes.

The Planet of Junior Brown, which airs tomorrow night on CBC, is the filmmaker's first feature for television. Once again Clement unearths magical properties in the number three: Like *Rude*, *Planet* mingles the stories of a trio of black characters. Based on the award-winning novel by Virginia Hamilton, the film follows the relationship between the sensitive, musically-gifted Junior (Martin Villafana) a kindly street kid named Buddy (Rainbow Sun Francks) and their eccentric school janitor, Mr. Pool (Clark Johnson). Junior and Buddy find wonder, refuge and acceptance in a secret room in the school basement where Mr. Pool has constructed a spectacular model of a ten-planet solar system.

Throughout the film, Buddy attempts to prevent the emotionally neglected Junior from retreating even further into his own fantasy world. At the same time, Buddy must maintain order on his own "planet," the abandoned building where he and other homeless youths dwell.

The movie unfolds as a redemptive fairy tale, but don't come expecting a straightforward storyline. "The way I experience the world is not in the classic Hollywood way," says Virgo. "For me, the non-linear approach to storytelling resonates more."

What's a Black Critic to Do? ~ 37

If Clement Virgo decided to make a movie of his life it might begin something like this: "I'd probably start when my brother was born. I was four, and my parents told me that babies came from helicopters. I lived near an army base in Jamaica and helicopters were always flying over. So one day, when my mother showed up with this baby, I just assumed the helicopter brought him."

The less imaginative of us, however, might begin like this: Clement Virgo was born in Kingston, Jamaica in 1966 to a shoemaker and a nurse's aide. His mother had educational aspirations for her children so she moved herself, Virgo, his brother and two sisters to Toronto. Virgo's father opted to remain behind.

Virgo doesn't have much to say about his early years in Toronto, except that his teachers seemed perversely eager to push him into carpentry. Instead, he landed a job with Harry Rosen creating window displays. To occupy his evenings, he enrolled in a film course at Ryerson Polytechnical Institute where he met independent filmmaker Virginia Rankin. The pair wound up collaborating on *A Small Dick Fleshy Ass Thang*, a short film that peeked in on a black man and a white woman in bed arguing about their body parts. In 1991, Virgo was accepted into the Canadian Film Centre's full-time program. The resulting film, *Save My Lost Nigga' Soul*, was named Best Short Film at both the Toronto and Chicago film festivals in 1993.

Because of the international acclaim for *Rude*, perhaps, Virgo was able to dodge the label of "black director" and is primarily known as a Canadian director. Still, no matter how well he renders his characters, Virgo believes that there is a limit to the number of movies that can feature non-white protagonists. "I think white people will see a film (about non-whites) if it's filtered through a white eye. Like Brad Pitt taking them through Tibet.

"I know when I'm watching a movie and a black person comes on the screen, my attention really pops up. So, for instance, when Sam shows up in Casablanca, I want him to be part of the whole thing. But it breaks my heart when I see him carrying Humphrey Bogart's bags and calling him 'Boss.' It breaks my heart."

Perhaps the most-commented upon aspect of Virgo's work is his impressionistic handling of light, and *The Planet of Junior Brown* is just one extraordinary example. Set in Toronto during the holiday season, the film possesses a gentle incandescence. One of the most powerful shots catches Buddy's girlfriend Butter (Sarah Polley), crouched in the shadow of a wall, robotically repeating requests for change. Scenes like that evoke visceral rather than intellectual responses, which is exactly what Virgo set out to achieve.

"I don't ever want to lecture or preach," he says. "I want the audience to have real emotions, not false or forced emotions.

"Some of my favourite filmmakers try and do that," he adds. "Look at Frank Capra and *It's a Wonderful Life*. I like Frank Capra because he has an honesty and an optimism. I think that ultimately I'm a pretty optimistic guy." [*Globe and Mail*, 1997]

In the Garden

I have just finished reading *My Garden (Book):* (1999) by Jamaica Kincaid. In it Kincaid has gathered together her own wonderfully idiosyncratic thoughts about the gardening life and the thing that strikes me most about this collection is just how happy—even blissful—she sounds. Happy and blissful are not the kind of words generally used to describe Kincaid or her work. Her best known novels *Annie John* (1986) and *The Autobiography of My Mother* (1996) explore the profound alienation of her West Indian heroines. Her memoir, *My Brother* (1997), chronicles her younger sibling's struggle with AIDS. Her extended essay, *A Small Place*, addresses political corruption in her native Antigua. Both *My Brother* and *A Small Place* envelop the reader in an atmosphere of Faulknerian decay.

Even the engaging collection of gardening essays published in *The New Yorker* in the early 1990s sound a plaintive note, expounding as they do upon the sorry relationship between the history of botany and the history of colonial conquest. *My Garden (Book):* incorporates the *New Yorker* pieces. One of the points Kincaid takes pains to highlight, is that this pleasure and privilege of gardening, of cultivating plants from around the world in one's own backyard, comes at great cost to someone somewhere else. For example, the feathery dahlia so popular here in North America, only comes to us as a consequence of Spain's conquest of Mexico. And that likewise the bougainvillea and Bermuda Lily found in her native Antigua are indigenous to South America and Japan.

It is Kincaid's fidelity to sad historical fact that has led her to publicly declare that she can never be completely happy. Indeed she believes that no responsible person ought ever to be completely happy. As she told a reporter from *Mother Jones* magazine:

> You can't have this luxury of pleasure without someone paying for it. This is nice to know. It's nice to know that when you sit down to enjoy a plate of strawberries, somebody got paid very little so that you could have your strawberries. It doesn't mean the strawberries will taste different, but it's nice to enjoy things less than we do. We enjoy things far too much and it leads to incredible pain and suffering.

All the same, Kincaid's allusions to the brutalities of botany do nothing to suppress the joy that spurts like a geyser from the pages of *My*

Garden (Book): where she is speaking to us directly, or so it seems, from the middle of a flower bed on her three and a half acres of farmland in the village of Bennington, Vermont:

> Is there someone to whom I can write for an answer to this question: Why is my wisteria floribunda, trained into a standard so that it will eventually look like a small tree, blooming in late July, almost August, instead of May, the way wisterias in general are supposed to do? The one that is blooming out of its natural season is blue in color; I have another one similiar in every way (or so I believe), except that it should show white flowers: it does not bloom at all, it only throws out long, twining stems, mixing itself up with the canes of the Rosa Alchymist, which is growing not too nearby, mixing itself up with a honeysuckle (Lonicera) and even going far away to twine itself around a red rose (Rosa Henry Kelsy). What do do? I like to ask myself this question, What to do? Especially when I myself do not have an answer to it. What to do?

A little later on she adds:

> How agitated I am when I am in the garden, and how happy I am to be so agitated. How vexed I am when I am in the garden, and how happy I am to be so vexed.

From the Royal Botanical Gardens annual show in Chelsea Kincaid writes:

> I was in a daze because I was among so many exquisite flowers and because I was in the midst of people who were so pleasant and kind it was hard to believe they were related to the people who were so rude and insulting to me as I passed through customs. If you ever want to keep up a grudge against someone, don't see that person at the Chelsea Flower Show standing among rhodendrons in impossible shades of mauve, pink and peach.

Perhaps you have already gleaned the most important thing about Kincaid's work: her dogged pursuit of the truth, particularly when it comes to the topics that absorb her most, her West Indian heritage and her love of flowers.

And this dogged pursuit of truth carries its own technical implications. Her prose style comes across as a pure and simple reflection of the workings of her mind. It follows the mind's natural rhythms, which is to say that it is full of parenthetical thoughts and parallels and repetitions.

At the same time her narratives possess a tautness, like a violin string tightened and tuned; both give an impression of tonal quality, elegance and control.

Paradoxically, Kincaid's voice comes across as childlike and unrestrained. Her observations are at once guileless and pointed. Her criticisms about Antigua, for example, have been the source of great displeasure to her fellow countrymen who complain that she is about the business of discrediting her people.

It is true that Kincaid's remarks are often painful and antagonizing. Like the time she shared with me her disdain for the Antiguan government.

"Antiguans are locked in shame," she explained, "over a situation in which their own people, who look like them, are now more cruel to them and have less pity on them, than the former colonial government."

A general outcry followed the publication of *A Small Place*, a non-fiction account of her island's people and politics. She told me that one evening after a reading, an Antiguan woman approached her to object.

"What you say is true," she said. "But do you have to say it?"

I find Kincaid's observations bracing. For one thing they are truly original, by which I mean they are her own, and I don't believe, as some people do, that they are calculated to shock. Perhaps she is aware that they might shock, but she can hardly help that. Besides people should be shocked by the situations she describes, not by the fact she describes them.

These days most people who flatter themselves into believing they are being original really have nothing new or interesting to say, rather they thrive on being rude or incorrect. But Kincaid does not mistake rudeness for cleverness. At the same time she is absolutely not about to adhere to a literary etiquette she finds stultifying and foolish. One of the reasons *My Garden (Book):* is such a delight to read is that Kincaid is heedless in asserting her likes and dislikes. She names names. She loves the Ronniger's seed catalogue for its simple newsprint advertisements and then she hates the White Farm Flower Catalogue because its glossy pictures look so conceited. But then, even though she hates the White Farm catalogue, she cannot resist purchasing some platycodon and campanula and Canada lilies, because the White Farm's glossy pictures make them look so good.

For Jamaica Kincaid, the garden equals memories of home. One day while looking over her many oddly-shaped flower beds in her Bennington yard, she realized she had unconsciously created a map of the West Indies.

Gardens didn't much exist on the island of Antigua while Kincaid was growing up. Most ordinary people—people of African descent—required their outdoor spaces to cook and eat and wash. If you did have a garden, it was an indication that you were well-off, that you had a spacious home, and that you could keep your yard for leisure. Kincaid remembers a family friend who had her own rose garden; on special occasions her mother would send her to request a bouquet. Another family had a willow tree in its front yard. At Christmas they would shape it into a pine and decorate it with ornaments and lights.

Kincaid had a large tree outside her house as well. She remembers being forced to sit beneath it whenever she was bad.

Kincaid's favourite garden memory recalls an idyllic period, the days before her childhood seemed to abruptly conclude. She was 9 years old and her stepfather, suffering from a heart ailment, was home from work. Jamaica, who was a little under the weather, had been kept back from school for several days. During their convalescence the two walked each day to the botanical gardens. After her stepfather had snipped some myrtle bush to brew his special tea, they would curl up beneath the rubber tree. He told her stories about the parents who had abandoned him when he was small:

> It was in the shade of the distorted branches of the rubber tree (though this distortion is perfectly natural to the rubber tree) in the botanical garden of St. John's, Antigua, a garden that was the creation of the most ambivalent of people, that I came to know important things, though I came to understand them only long after. Not the least of which is how I became a writer. My father: his mother left him when he was a small child, small enough for it to matter so much to him that he still spoke of it when he was over fifty years old, but of course it turns out that no matter what time your mother leaves you, it always matters: she went to England and he never saw her again. She once sent him a pair of shoes, but they were too big and they were put away; when he tried them on again, he had outgrown them. Perhaps at the same time, (perhaps before, perhaps afterward, it was never made clear to me), his father left him and went off to build the Panama Canal. If my father knew then that his own father had not single-handedly built the Panama Canal, he did not make it clear to me.

Who among us understands the magic of the writing process? Clearly her stepfather's story transplanted itself in Kincaid's imagination where it mingled among the seminal events of her own life, and blossomed into the theme that would become central to her novels—the theme of a maternal abandonment. Kincaid's first novel, *Annie John*, tells of an Antiguan girl whose journey through adolescence estranges her from her mother. Her second novel, *Lucy* (1990), begins where *Annie John* leaves off. Lucy moves to America to work as an au pair, relieved to be far from her mother.

Kincaid is not one of those authors who try to convince you that nothing they write is autobiographical. Rather she asserts that she is always writing autobiographically, always trying to work out the painful facts of life between her mother and herself. In *My Brother*, she writes about their troubled relationship. She records her efforts to support her family throughout the crisis. At the same time, *My Brother* provides a tortured account of the events that drove Kincaid and her mother apart.

Jamaica Kincaid was born Elaine Potter Richardson in St. John's, Antigua on May 25, 1949. Her mother Annie Richardson immigrated to Antigua from Dominica at the age of 16. Annie was not married to Jamaica's father, Roderick Potter, whom Jamaica has described as a certain type of West Indian man. Potter took little interest in the dozen or so children he sired all around the island.

In any case, Jamaica did not learn that her mother's husband, David Drew, was not her biological father until she was grown. She adored her stepfather and the feeling was mutual. As a child, she adored her mother as well. She did not for a moment doubt that she was well-loved. Her mother would do anything for her. Whenever Jamaica complained that she was too tired to eat, her mother would chew the food herself before placing it in her daughter's mouth. Every morning Annie washed the child's feet in urine, an obeah ritual that protected her from evil. Annie Richardson shared with her daughter her love for reading and flowers, two passions that would remain with Jamaica for life.

But the bond between mother and daughter frayed as Jamaica entered adolescence. By then three more children had arrived: Joseph, Dalma and Devon. With three toddlers and an increasingly ailing husband, Annie turned to her young daughter for domestic support. Annie expected Jamaica to relinquish her childish concerns and share in the house-work and childrearing duties.

Not surprisingly, furious confrontations ensued. Annie grew so frustrated with Jamaica's continual reading that she burned all of the girl's books. She pulled Jamaica out of school just as she was ready to try her "O" level exams, and pushed her to go abroad. Annie wanted her to find a job that would enable her to send money home.

Jamaica did leave, as we know, but fuelled by rage and resentment. Her stories shimmer with the heat of a hostility that continues to burn between the two.

Who among us can claim to understand the magic of the writing process? Perhaps Kincaid mused over her sense of emotional abandonment and perhaps she mused over her stepfather's story of abandonment as well. And perhaps she extrapolated from these two situations that abandonment was somehow central to the West Indian experience. Of course, if you are of West Indian descent, as I am, this is a painful issue to deliberate. But once I did, I began to recall the various writers who had shared with me their stories of abandonment. The author Dionne Brand was two when her mother went off to England to become a nurse. She left Dionne in Trinidad with her grandmother and aunts. When her grandmother passed away a decade later, Brand's mother returned. But it was too late for them to build a relationship, Brand says. They couldn't get along.

And then there is the writer Cecil Foster, author of *A Place Called Heaven: The Meaning of Being Black in Canada* (2002) and *No Man in the House* (1991). Foster and his brothers were raised by their grandmothers in Barbados. His parents had gone to England as well, where they hoped to find good jobs. They promised to send for their sons once they were properly settled. Foster spent his entire childhood waiting to join his parents. But the call never came.

Kincaid has named the act of abandonment as one that marks the West Indian condition. From there to Africa's abandonment of its own people is not too great a leap. Kincaid is one of a few black writers brave enough to voice the shameful truth that Africans sold other Africans into slavery. No wonder then, that when Kincaid thinks about flowers her mind settles on the forcible removal of plants from their native homes. And no wonder she focuses on their dispersion throughout the various colonial empires. Nor is it surprising that she preoccupies herself with questions of cultivation and adaptation. She cannot help but notice that Africa's displaced flora has adjusted far better than her dislocated people.

Kincaid manages these themes deftly in her novel *The Autobiography of My Mother* in which she draws a parallel between her own ambivalence towards her mother and the West Indian's ambivalence towards Africa. By Africa, Kincaid does not refer so much to the continent itself but to its culture, belief systems, ways of being. In *The Autobiography of My Mother* Kincaid explores West Indians' profound alienation from themselves.

Jamaica Kincaid once described herself as a very colonial person. Even so, from an early age she rebelled against the experience. When she was a schoolgirl of 9 or 10 she refused to stand up to sing "God Save the King." She also despised the anthem, "Rule Btitannia," especially the chorus:

Rule Brittania
Rule the waves,
We Britons never ever
Shall be slaves.

Jamaica found the song ridiculous, since she and her classmates weren't British, and since they were the descendants of slaves. She was forever asking, "What has this to do with me?"

She resented having to memorize the romantic poets. She developed a particular distaste for Wordsworth's "I Wandered Lonely As a Cloud," a poem about daffodils. To this day, she claims to dislike daffodils and even to dislike their particular shade of yellow.

Nevertheless, years of studying the British classics leave their impression. *The Autobiography of My Mother* is the story of a girl, who like Jane Austen's Emma or Charlotte Brontë's Lucy Snow, must make her way without the guidance and sheltering love of a mother. Of course, Kincaid's heroines lack the advantages that naturally accrue to upper and middle class English white women. She examines the experiences of a black woman whose island world props up the privileged British system.

The Autobiography of My Mother is set on the island of Dominica where Xuela Claudette Desvereaux loses her mother as soon as she is born. Her mother dies during childbirth and the bereavement casts Xuela into a state of emotional isolation by which she defines herself for the rest of her life.

Xuela's father is a representative of the colonial government who works his way up through the ranks. When his wife dies he does not know what to do with the child. It is apparently inconceivable that he might raise her. In the end he hands Xuela over to his laundress in much the same way he hands over his dirty clothes. He sees his daughter every fortnight when he delivers his shirts for cleaning. These brief visits, more like sightings, comprise Xuela's relationship with her father.

The laundress is named Eunice and although Xuela lives with Eunice from birth she never feels at home. It's not that Eunice is a bad person. Eunice does not feel any particular affection for Xuela, but then she doesn't feel any affection for her own children either. She cleans them and feeds them and does what she is expected to do, but Eunice reserves her real love for her few material possessions, especially a bone china plate featuring a painted scene of an English meadow. When Xuela accidentally breaks this plate Eunice collapses with grief. She punishes the child by forcing her to kneel on a pile of stones in the hot sun holding heavy rocks over her head.

Eunice's choice of punishment conjures images of slavery. But this abusive behaviour is not the reason Xuela can never feel comfortable in Eunice's home. Xuela cannot feel comfortable with any woman who steps in to replace her mother, for she sees any such figure as illegitimate. The laundress is the first of three surrogate mothers Xuela's father provides. He fails to realize that these substitute women cannot erase Xuela's sense of loss.

Then again, Xuela's feelings are not really an issue for Alfred. He would never understand her desire for natural ties; as a representative of the Crown he has casually cast aside links to his African heritage in order to further the British tradition. Alfred is dark-skinned, but is in fact of mixed heritage. His father was a Scot, his mother of African descent. His father abandons the family to return to the land of his birth. Yet it is his father's culture Alfred looks to for validation.

When Xuela is about 10, Alfred remarries and Xuela moves into the home he shares with his new wife. It is the first time father and daughter have lived together. Unfortunately, Xuela's stepmother sees her as a threat. The woman despises the girl and even attempts to kill her. She places a curse on a necklace and then gives it to Xuela as a present. But Xuela's intuition tells her not to wear the necklace. Instead she puts it around the neck of her stepmother's dog which falls down dead in a matter of hours. Life improves for Xuela after her father and stepmother have children of their own.

When Xuela enters puberty her father sends her away to school. This time he places her in the care of a woman named Madame La Batte. For the first time, Xuela is showered with kindess, although Madame La Batte has ulterior motives. She wants to offer Xuela's ripening body as a gift to her husband. Monsieur La Batte has not made love to his wife in years. Madame La Batte hopes an affair with Xuela will keep him close to home.

Xuela is not dismayed by La Batte's sexual advances and finds herself longing to be with him at night. Their affair might have continued indefinitely had she not discovered she was pregnant. Xuela is horrified by her predicament. She steals money from La Batte to pay for an abortion. A medicine woman serves Xuela a thick black liquid. After several agonizing days, the foetus aborts itself.

I have often heard people from the West Indies say how good it is to come from a part of the world where most everyone is black; what an advantage it is over the North American experience. But in *The Autobiography of My Mother* the absence of white people only intensifies colour consciousness. Even though Xuela is surrounded by people who are black like her, she is encouraged to believe they are somehow inferior: When Xuela's father sends her off to school he warns her about the other students.

Says Xuela:

> We were not friends, such a thing was discouraged. We were never to trust each other. This was like a motto repeated to us by our parents; it was a part of my upbringing, like a form of good manners. You cannot trust these people, my father would say to me, the very words the other children's parents were saying to them, perhaps even at the same time. That these people were ourselves, that this insistence of mistrust of others, that people who looked so very much like each other, who shared a common history of suffering and humiliation and enslavement, should be taught to mistrust each other, even as children, is no longer a mystery to me. The people we should naturally have mistrusted were beyond our influence completely; what we needed to defeat them, to rid ourselves of them, was something far more powerful than mistrust. To mistrust each other was just one of the many feelings we had for each other, all of them the opposite of love, all of them standing in the place of love. It was as if we were in competition with each other for a secret prize and we were afraid that someone else would get it.

The islanders' ambivalence towards themselves as black people causes them to doubt their traditional beliefs. An incident from Xuela's childhood elucidates the problem. One day when Xuela and her school-mates are walking to school they see a striking woman in the middle of the river. She is naked, beautiful with dark brown skin and shiny black hair, and she is surrounded by all kinds of delicious-looking fruits. She is so lovely that the children suspect she is not a real person and they warn one another to keep their distance.

However, one boy is tantalized. He cannot stop himself from swimming toward the woman. He swims and he swims but he never seems to reach her. Finally he grows exhausted and sinks beneath the waters. He disappears and is never seen again. Most of the children recognize the woman as a dangerous apparition. But as they grow older they begin to doubt what they have seen.

"They no longer believe what they saw with their own eyes," says Xuela, "or in their own reality. This is no longer without an explanation to me. Everything about us is held in doubt and we the defeated define all that is unreal, all that is not human, all that is without love, all that is without mercy. Our experience cannot be interpreted by us; we do not know the truth of it.

Our God was not the correct one, our understanding of heaven and hell was not a respectable one. Belief in that apparition of a naked woman with outstretched arms beckoning a small boy to his death was the belief of the illegitimate, the poor, the low. I believe in that apparition then and I believe in it now."

What would have happened to African people under colonial rule, Kincaid has sometimes wondered, if they had held on to their own systems of belief? In *The Autobiography of My Mother* the Dominicans' ambivalence about their heritage leaves them as vulnerable as Xuela's physical estrangement from her past. "Who am I?" Xuela repeatedly asks herself. "My mother is dead."

Part of the power of the novel is that Kincaid takes the discussion of colonialism beyond race. Colonialism is colour-coded to be sure, and Kincaid thoroughly emphasizes the dominance of white people over black. But at the same time, she implies that the desire for superiority is an innate characteristic of human nature. Xuela's mother, like Kincaid's mother, is half Carib Indian, and one of the last remaining members of her people. As Xuela puts it, "Africans are the defeated who have survived, while Caribs are the defeated who are extinct." Black characters who recognize the Indian cast of Xuela's features are often anxious to denigrate her.

Kincaid's novel examines sexism as well as racism. While Xuela is clearly more intelligent than her ineffectual half brother, he is the one who will inherit her father's wealth. Yet this is not a concern for Xuela. She wants no part of the riches acquired through her father's association with the British. Xuela's half sister feels differently, however. She grows sad and bitter with the knowledge that her parents favour her brother.

Even romantic relationships contain a power dynamic. Xuela falls in love with a handsome stevedore named Roland. Xuela's feelings for Roland are intense. Unfortunately Roland's wife shares her sentiments, accosting Xuela in the street, and calling her every kind of bad name. Xuela responds with neither anger nor guilt. She does not believe that she has wronged any one and she does not feel that she has been wronged.

In any case her love for Roland does not last forever. Xuela falls in love and then she falls out of love. She is essentially a solitary being, uninterested in owning another. "The impulse to possess is alive in every heart," she remarks. "Some people choose vast plains, some people choose high mountains, some people choose wide seas and some people choose husbands. I choose to possess myself."

Indeed, *The Autobiography of My Mother* is the chronicle of Xuela's quest to know and love herself. It is the story of how she achieves this state without any of the crucial advantages life offers—without a mother to love her and assure her of her value and without a culture to validate her past and her present.

Xuela is overwhelmingly successful. Indeed, this ability to empower oneself without validation from the world, is one of the most salient features of black women's writing. For the most part, Xuela learns to love herself by instinct. It is a long process. First, she embraces everything she is told to hate—she learns to love the dirt behind her ears and even the various smells of her body. In time she comes to understand, control and enjoy her own sexuality.

But it is during a period of self-imposed exile that Xuela develops a deep and sustaining self-love. After leaving school she sells her few possessions and rents a small house. She takes a job repairing roads. She cuts her hair short and adopts an androgynous appearance. She follows a lonely daily routine. Time for contemplation brings her to an awareness of herself. "I came to know myself and this frightened me," she says. "To rid myself of this fear I began to look at a reflection of my face in any surface I could find; a still pool on the shallow banks of the river became my most common mirror."

From the start of the novel Xuela feels utterly alone, which is strange, in a way, as her father is always near by. She and Alfred are not especially close, but he shows her greater regard than many fathers do. He makes certain she has shelter, and provides her with an extensive education, almost unheard of for a black girl. And Xuela does love her father. She worries about him and misses him from time to time, especially after his death.

Yet because of his identification with the oppressor, Alfred fails to teach Xuela life's most important lesson, which is how to love oneself. Xuela might have learned this lesson from her mother, but Xuela's mother is dead.

I wonder if it is alright to go out on a limb and suggest that Kincaid may be saying something significant about West Indian men and about black men in general. Perhaps she is suggesting that their deep desire to prove themselves in white society results in a profound abandonment of their children, for which the physical act of desertion is only a metaphor. At any rate, Xuela does not blame her father for identifying with the colonizer, for in so doing he proves himself "commonly human":

> My father rejected the complications of the vanquished; he chose the complications of the victor. In the vanquished, had he looked he would have felt the blankness all human beings are confronted with day after day, a blankness they hope to fill and sometimes succeed in filling, but then again, mostly not.

Xuela describes the isolation and ambivalence of the human condition in the same language she uses to describe her own isolation and abandonment at the start of the novel. She says, "at my end there was nothing, no one between me and the black room of the world."

Jamaica Kincaid is the last person that comes to mind when one thinks of the negro spirituals, those plangent cries of brutalized slaves to a distressingly invisible God. All the same, she sees the black person as a motherless child, a long way from home. [Toronto Public Library, Spring 2000]

Black Man's Burden

In his home in Thornhill, on the outskirts of Toronto, Barbadian-Canadian writer Cecil Foster is attempting to subdue the exuberant antics of his 3-year-old son Mensah. The two play near the fireplace, where more than a dozen pint-sized trophies are lined up along the mantelpiece. They belong to Foster's two older sons, 13-year-old Michello and 14-year-old Munyonzwe, recognition of their achievements in competitive swimming and soccer. These prizes, along with the boys' courteous demeanour, suggest that they are confident, well-adjusted children, secure of their place in the community. Yet Foster wonders: "Will my children ever be accepted as fully Canadian?"

For Foster, 42, the question is answered by another: "Could one of his three sons ever become Prime Minister?" The query is largely rhetorical. But in his new book, *A Place Called Heaven: The Meaning of Being Black in Canada*, Foster argues that deeply entrenched and growing Canadian racism dampens even the most seemingly attainable dreams, effectively thwarting the sense of belonging of an entire community.

Foster, a former business journalist, with two novels to his credit, offers a provocative synthesis of the personal and the political. Most of the book is devoted to the experiences of a broad cross-section of black Canadians. The head of the Federal Court of Canada, Grenada-born Chief Justice Julius Isaac, dismisses notions that his high-ranking position translates into significant influence for the black community. And Ontario Liberal MPP Alvin Curling wryly discusses his term as the lone black member of former Ontario Premier David Peterson's cabinet. Foster also takes readers inside the Toronto jail to paint a uniquely humane portrait of Clinton Gayle, the Jamaican-born, Canadian raised man convicted in the shooting death of Toronto police officer Todd Baylis. The author sees the media's fixation on Gayle's Jamaican background as evidence of mainstream racist attitudes.

Foster's opinion that racism is on the increase relies rather heavily upon personal opinion and observation—he includes numerous anecdotes about police harassment and education inequities—but minimally upon statistics. In addition, the book contains some inexplicably faulty editing. In spite of these weaknesses, Foster presents a provocative argument. He devotes particular scrutiny to the Greater Toronto area, where, according to a 1992 Multiculturalism and Citizenship Canada study, more than three quarters of the country's roughly half a million black people reside, and where 83% of them earn less than $25,000 a year.

As the ultimate destination for freedom-seeking African-American slaves, Canada has always held a special place in the hearts of people of African descent. But Foster notes the emergence of a terrible double irony: not only has the image of Canada as a land of equity nearly disintegrated, but America—the very country once disparaged as the bastion of racism—now provides greater opportunities, at least for blacks of Caribbean descent. Statistics place the earnings of Caribbean-born males in the US second only to that of white males. Foster further lists Americans of Caribbean heritage among the country's leading political figures, including the former head of the Joint Chief of Staff, Colin Powell.

Foster was born in Barbados. He and his two brothers were raised by their two grandmothers after their parents emigrated to England. He worked as a journalist before arriving in Canada in 1979, where he eventually landed positions at the *Toronto Star* and the *Globe and Mail*, and later became a senior editor at the *Financial Post*. His first novel, *No Man In The House*, appeared in 1991 and his second *Sleep On, Beloved* in 1994.

These days Foster shares his views on current affairs as a columnist for the *Toronto Star* and, for the past year, as host of a talk show on Toronto's biggest station CFRB. He not infrequently espouses ideas that irritate his black listeners, such as his opposition to the concept of black-focused schools. Many blacks protested his decision to join the staff of CFRB in the first place, a station the community has traditionally perceived as stoking anti-black, anti-immigrant sentiment. "CFRB has a history they have to deal with," Foster says. "But quite a number of blacks listen to the station and now they are no longer voyeurs."

Foster maintains that Canadian racism is extremely tenacious, but he is optimistic that it can be diminished through frank discussion, and some aggressive political maneuvering. His audacious solution for the inclusion and the empowerment of black Canadians is a bold power play on the part of Quebec blacks, who he believes have just enough voting power to close the gap between the federalists and separatists. He suggests that Quebec's 110,000-strong black population support whichever party agrees to enter into constitutional discussions with black Canadians to determine which policies might best serve their community. "I don't think it's cynical," says Foster. "We have entered into an era of self-interest. Blacks have a long history in this country that goes back to the Empire Loyalists and even further in Quebec. We can force the federal government to make us feel wanted." [*Maclean's*, 1996]

The Homecoming

Sometime during the winter of 1978, Marie Laferrière learned from a friend in the Haitian military that her 23-year-old son, Dany, was on the short list for imprisonment or death. It was during the bloody regime of Jean Claude (Baby Doc) Duvalier, who like his father before him, the tyrannical François, sought to eradicate all opposition. Dany, a journalist, refrained from political commentary—he specialized in witty observations of village life. Yet officials saw a threat in his growing popularity.

Marie wasted no time procuring the necessary travel documents. She knew the drill, for she had lost her husband to exile two decades before. Only when Dany's papers were in order did she confess to him that his life was in danger. She apprised him of his imminent departure. He would escape to Montreal.

In *Down Among the Dead Men* (1997), an autobiographical book, Dany Laferrière chronicles a recent return to the country of his birth and to the mother he has not seen in twenty years. On arrival he finds a brutalized people occupying a ghoulish landscape that is marked by drought and decay. His mother's home at least is a comforting sanctuary. It lies outside Port-au-Prince in Carrefour Feuilles, at the top of Nelhio Hill, an incline so steep cab drivers must be bribed to attempt it.

Actually, this is not Laferrière's first time back in Haiti. He returned briefly in 1993 for a couple of television spots. But he had to leave quickly without seeing his mother, who, in any case, remained fearful for his life. The stopover hardly qualified as a homecoming: "For me Haiti is something very specific and very precious," Laferrière says in charming, uncertain English on a recent lunch date in Toronto. "Haiti is my mother, my aunt. I love them because they are exactly like my country. They begin with so much promise and so much joy. Then they struggle for a long while and feel like a failure. Yet this is when they become even stronger."

Although Laferrière identifies strongly with his native country, he will never be classified as a principally Haitian writer. His two adopted countries, Canada and the US, have embraced him as their own. His first book, the unforgettable and unforgettably titled *How To Make Love To A Negro Without Getting Tired* (1985), guaranteed him a previously uninhabited literary niche. It offered an amusing account of a black man's intimate relationships with white women at McGill University in Montreal. Laferrière returns to this early period in another newly released memoir called *A Drifting Year*.

Most critics dismissed his second novel *Eroshima* (1987), while *An Aroma of Coffee* (1991), Laferrière's exquisite evocation of the summer he spent with his grandmother, introduced readers to his gentler side. With *Why Must a Black Writer Write About Sex?* (1994) and *Dining With The Dictator* (1994) Laferrière recapitulated the themes of sex and power that had secured his reputation.

Despite his preoccupation with the prurient, Laferrière, a lanky, ebullient, dark-skinned man, admits to being very "bourgeois." He is still in love with the wife he met in Montreal in 1979. They live most of the year in Miami, where Laferrière hosts a French-language radio program, and where the couple are raising their three girls aged 17, 12 and 7. When Laferrière talks about his daughters, his chest actually swells: "I am just like King Lear," he says, with a hearty laugh.

Down Among the Dead Men is filled with the author's droll satire and often scabrous wit. Of course, nothing could be less amusing than the Haiti Laferrière describes, where decades of political corruption and barbarism have led to turmoil and rot. The air around Port-au-Prince is rank with the sickly sweet of over-ripeness. Human excrement lines the beach in Carrefour where new latrines have not been built. Life throughout the capital verges on the macabre, particularly the terrifying rumour that the country's over-crowded cemeteries have emptied out. Even the intellectuals believe that the dead have re-entered the world.

Yet Laferrière can't help but celebrate the idiosyncrasies that even in the midst of crisis affirm the Haitian life. In one example, Laferrière renders a hilarious cab ride in which the driver makes several unanticipated stops to pay child support to the mothers of his apparently countless children. "It's true," Laferrière said, "Haiti is a dead country. But it is also the most lively country in the world. You just have to see the painting, the music, the women, the men...the appetite for life."

The tension between the author's animated portrayal of the Haitian spirit and the country's dire circumstances infuses Laferrière's prose with quirky humour. Yet Laferrière denies that he sets out to inspire laughter.

"I don't use humour so much," he said. "I don't try to be funny. I am funny because you are funny. You find what you bring."

He sticks to this interpretation even though it was his subtle lampoonery that forced him out of Haiti in the first place. Duvalier officials considered him a taunt. Laferrière explains, with characteristic deadpan: "The government was thinking 'We do not understand what this guy is saying, but we know it is something against us!' The good school of dictatorship," he adds with a nod.

Laferrière's departure from Haiti twenty years ago may have been sudden, but he harbours no regrets. He had always planned to see the world. He also felt it was time to put some distance between himself and a loving, but overprotective mother: "She thought she should still give me my bath at 23."

Even so, Laferrière stayed away much longer than intended. When he finally arrived back in Port-au-Prince, his mother and aunt could hardly breathe for excitement. Says Laferrière, "They danced a circle around me, clapping their hands and singing, 'He's back home again! He's back home again!'" [*Globe and Mail*, 1998]

I Remember Papa

I went to visit Rachel Manley one afternoon at her home in Toronto. It was a brilliant day. The afternoon sun spilled through the kitchen window, trailed through the dining room and formed pale shadows in the drawing room beyond where Manley lay stretched out on a plump white sofa, a heavy quilt pulled up to her chin. She explained to me that the furnace was giving trouble and that she felt cold. But one could also see that she was tired. The festivities of the previous evening had left her drained.

The night before, her latest book *Slipstream: A Daughter Remembers* (2000) had been launched at Toronto's Arts and Letters Club. *Slipstream* is a memoir, a poignant chronicle of the loving, conflicted relationship she shared with her father, former Jamaican Prime Minister Michael Manley. Manley died of cancer in 1997 at the age of 72. Rachel began writing *Slipstream* during the final months of his life. It is the second installment in the trilogy that began with *Drumblair: Memories of a Jamaican Childhood* (1997), her personal recollections of her grandparents, Jamaica's first chief minister Norman Washington Manley and his artistic wife, Edna.

Among the crowd of well-wishers at the Arts and Letters Club an attitude of reverent nostalgia prevailed, vanquishing, for the moment, lingering bitterness about Michael Manley's socialist policies. During the 1970s those policies had led many Jamaicans to flee the island for dubious comforts abroad. Manley read aloud from her book with Granville "Jack" Johnson, her father's trusted comrade, by her side. When she momentarily lost her place, Johnson broke into a rendition of "Jamaica Arise," as he had so often done in her father's day:

> The trumpet has sounded
> My countrymen all.
> So awake from your slumber
> And answer the call.

His listeners joined in. Their voices thick with longing, pride and regret.

> The torch has been lighted
> The dawn is at hand.
> Who joins in the fight
> For his own native land.

"Last night wasn't business as usual," Manley whispered from her cocoon on the couch. "I didn't feel like it was a do that had been put on and that people were attending. When Jack stood there and sang...I could just remember the whole 1970s, the elections and all the hope. The evening was so emotional for me."

And lonely. Gone is the trinity of loved ones that for so long formed Manley's emotional foundation. Both her grandparents have passed away. And with her father's recent death the most meaningful ties to Manley's past have dissolved. These days, she admits, "I feel like I'm in a pool and I can't feel the bottom."

The book launch proved especially difficult. "I don't think I've ever missed those three giants like I did last night," she said. "Just missed them. Missed them so much. All three of them. I felt this huge loneliness."

Rachel Manley is 53 years old and married, with two grown children (Drum and Luke) from two previous marriages. Yet she seems ageless in a Peter Pan sort of way. She is petite, a sprite, and seems light enough to defy gravity. She speaks with startling poetic candour and exudes such immediate warmth that I am surprised when she confides that loneliness is a feeling she has struggled with all her life. She attributes this to being separated from her mother, the first of her father's five wives, at an early age. The marriage ended when Manley was a toddler. Mother and daughter did not meet again for fourteen years.

"When you lose a mother at two," said Manley, "I think you are left with a slightly bereft feeling that you can't quite put your finger on. I'm always amazed at how many people wake up happy first thing in the morning. My waking up is always a process of getting busy so I don't brood."

Despite the devotion of her grandparents, Manley grew up perpetually lonely for the company of her father. In *Slipstream* Manley recounts her heart-wrenching efforts to hold his attention. But her father's climb to power—his heroic labour negotiations, his election to national office and the tumult of his political life—precluded the kind of father-daughter relationship Manley craved. What little personal space he allowed himself he committed largely to romance. Rachel found herself eagerly antici-pating his down times: "In a funny way, all my life, whenever my father was ill or heartbroken or defeated by an election, that was when I got him back. As I say in *Slipstream* ,'His troughs became my pinnacles.'"

It is a sad irony that the largest uninterrupted stretch Manley shared with her father occurred during his last months. Prostate cancer had left him bedridden in his unassuming Jamaican townhouse. Manley rarely left his side. Although she had originally set aside those weeks to work on her grandmother's biography, she realized that her father's story would have to come first: "I was just washed in the pain of my father (and) I gave in to it. I went through my old routine: when I woke and felt the pain, I just went to work and within five minutes of beginning writing I feel no pain. I am just weaving."

In *Slipstream* Manley expertly conveys the force and nobility of her father's character, even while he lies helpless in bed. Though the life seeps from his body, he remains "Michael Enormous," his spirit looms large. She also magnificently renders her own sorrow, which, by the end of the book, spins out into terror and rage. The final pages are a truly harrowing expression of grief.

"That was the bit that I wrote when he was still alive, when he was dying beside me," said Manley, her voice breaking slightly. "Not a word of it has been changed. From where it says 'Go to sleep, my beloved father, go to sleep. This is winter in the mountains.' I wrote that sitting beside him. What else could I do? I just sat there writing." [*Pride*, 2000]

The Music Man

When novelist Caryl Phillips enters a room, heads automatically turn. Strikingly handsome, the Yorkshire-raised novelist exhibits the hip self-assurance of the black star. At the same time he exudes charming British modesty. He is the literary equivalent of Mel and Denzel.

Not surprisingly, Phillips, whose new novel is *The Nature of Blood* (1997), has a reputation as a ladies' man, and he subtly dresses the part. He is wearing his trademark jeans, black shirt and charcoal sports jacket. His hair is closely cropped and geometrical, and his manners are impeccable.

The cool demeanour of the author reflects nothing of the passion of his novels, which deal with history's most horrific events. In 1993, *Crossing the River* received a nomination for the Booker Prize for its originality and artistry. The story told the diasporic experience of one enslaved African family over 250 years. Phillips employed individual contrasting voices to narrate the tale: black, white, male and female. *The Nature of Blood* also engages multiple voices. This time a chronicle of a racist fifteenth-century trial against Jews, and Othello's first-person account of life in Venice, amplify the brutal internment of a Jewish girl in a Nazi concentration camp.

Critics often compare Phillips's novels to blues and especially, jazz. "Music has always been really important to me," he says. "I have always regarded black musicians as the vanguard of African diasporic creativity. They gave me the most cultural strength. The other side of this, which has become more important to me as a writer, is technique. I've seen the way in which music often begins with one theme and then develops it. Jazz does this, classical music does this and now rap does it as well."

What is unique and controversial in Phillips is his desire to allow a variety of voices to be heard. He inhabits each of his characters—whether Victorian spinster, black slave or white master—with an eerie equality, a total absence of reserve. Phillips displays less interest in proving that the black man's experience is universal than in proving that the universal experience belongs to the black man.

Graham Swift, winner of the Booker Prize for his novel *Last Orders* (1996), has been friends with Phillips for more than a decade. In a recent telephone interview, Swift vividly recalled the first time the two met.

"It was at Harbourfront in Toronto in the hospitality suite, and all of a sudden the door opened very slowly and cautiously and this face

[Phillips'] peaked round," Swift said, laughing. "I thought to myself right away, 'I'm going to like this guy.'"

Phillips also smiles at the memory. This desire to size up people and situations is one that has served him well. He grew up near Leeds, England, where his parents, who are from St. Kitts in the West Indies, settled in 1958.

"At the time," says Phillips, "Leeds was an ugly town. It had dark, satanic buildings, black from soot. And it still looked as though there'd been a war lately, which, of course, there had." Phillips cannot forget the racism of the time and place. One minute, "you could be the star athlete and the next kids would be calling you 'nigger'."

"I realized when I was a teenager that I could read people better than my friends. I think it has a lot to do with the vigilance that is necessary if you are growing up in a society as an outsider; a society that has a peculiar attitude toward you."

"When I was in school my teachers told me all sorts of things, including what I couldn't do, and what I couldn't achieve, and I never believed them. I realized very quickly by just looking at them that they were speaking out of a spirit of a lack of generosity, or sometimes anger or sometimes just plain hate. I was able to read them.

"Originally I went to university to do psychology because I wanted to know about people. It never occurred to me that the best way of learning about people was (to study) literature."

At Oxford, Phillips began directing plays and, after he graduated, he began writing and directing his own works, which focused on the lives of contemporary black families in Britain. He attempted theatre before delving into writing novels because he felt comfortable with voice and dialogue. He wrote his first book, *The Final Passage*, in 1985.

Phillips spends about half his time in New York; the other half he spends at his home in London. Then he must also make space for the creative writing classes that he teaches each fall at Amherst College in Massachusetts where he is writer-in-residence. At one point he also had a home in St. Kitts, but he says now, "I'm scaling back."

He seems to thrive on a sense of physical freedom, as if the inability to pin him down to one geographic location works as safeguard for his creative, individualistic spirit. Nevertheless, his wanderlust has not prevented him from accumulating a number of fast, and famous, friends. Apart from Swift, there is Nobel laureate Derek Walcott, British novelist Margaret Drabble and Australian writer Peter Carey.

Like Phillips, novelist John Edgar Wideman teaches at Amherst College. On the line from Massachusetts, Wideman laughingly suggested that no party is complete without "Caz." All comments from Phillips' comrades are made with the barely contained, nefarious glee of libidinous high-school boys.

In 1995, Phillips travelled to Chicago and Atlanta to make a documentary film on singer-songwriter Curtis Mayfield, who was left a quadriplegic after a fluke accident on stage during an outdoor concert in 1990. Phillips speaks passionately about Mayfield, especially his gifts as a lyricist.

"In the '60s, pop songs were pop songs," he enthuses. "But then you have this man singing, "People get ready, there's a train a-comin'" and everything that that meant to black people. Just think. This was thirty years ago. It was amazing. The way the song said one thing to blacks and another to whites, who put it at the top of the Billboard Top 100. It was a double-edged sword.

"I'm absolutely fascinated with Mayfield," says Phillips. "I am fascinated by his ability to combine passion with social acumen." [*Globe and Mail*, 1997]

The Life of Portia White

My favourite picture of the famous black Canadian contralto, Portia White, was taken in June of 1941. In it Portia and four other girls stand in front of the Halifax School of Music, contestants in a festival. They are all dressed in the popular attire of the day; variations on a theme of the close-fitted shirtwaist paired with the A-line skirt. The four white girls are grouped together on the right. They smile tentatively into the lens. Portia, for some reason not immediately discernible, stands slightly apart. She does not smile, but directs towards the camera a detached gaze.

As I say, this is my favourite picture of Portia but it is probably not the photograph that pops into the minds of most people who recall the singing star celebrated for her moving renditions of German lieder and Negro spirituals. Haligonians in particular may best remember the resplendent image of Portia that accompanied rave reviews of her appearances at New York's prestigious Town Hall in 1944; or the glamorous studio portrait by the famed photographer Karsh; or perhaps they might recall the picture taken with Queen Elizabeth in 1964 after a performance in Charlottetown.

From 1942 to 1946 Portia White's hectic concert schedule swept her across Canada and the United States, and into Latin America and the Caribbean. Here at home people referred to Portia as "a credit to her race" which in the condescending racial discourse of the day was thought to be a great compliment.

Still, an odd sort of paradox was at work. At the same time that critics were applauding Portia's musical accomplishments, they were also diminishing the role she played in her own success. Article after article meted out an inordinate share of recognition to her teacher Ernesto Vinci and her patron Edith Read of Toronto and the Halifax Ladies Musical Club. To exacerbate this perception, articles from the 40s often describe the singer as a person of little motivation and less aspiration. Though Portia herself apparently played up this impression, it fails to ring true. She obviously harboured ambition enough to avoid domestic work, the chief career option available to black Canadian women.

In fact it is very likely that Portia possessed great expectations, if only because she had been profoundly influenced by her extraordinary father. Andrew White was a descendant of slaves who moved from Virginia to Truro, Nova Scotia in 1900, and married Izie Dora White (they shared the same last name) six years later. Reverend White was the first black man to graduate from Acadia University. Later he served as a chaplain for the British forces during the First World War.

When the family moved to Halifax in 1913 Reverend White took over leadership of the Cornwallis Street Baptist Church. Portia and her nine brothers and sisters made up the bulk of their father's choir. In the ensuing years she would take on the role of choir director and would perform on her father's weekly radio program to help Reverend White raise additional funds for his congregation.

By 1940, Portia, now a schoolteacher, was taking music lessons two and three evenings a week with the noted baritone Dr. Ernesto Vinci. Vinci had come to Halifax as a refugee from the war. His good friend Arturo Toscanini, director of the New York Symphony Orchestra, had helped him to land a position at the Halifax Conservatory as head of the vocal department. It was here that Vinci heard Portia sing for the first time: "Are there two Marian Andersons?" he is rumoured to have said, comparing her to the famed American contralto.

Under Vinci's tutelage Portia began to fulfill her potential. She won several provincial festivals, and local clubs and organizations started inviting her to perform at formal functions. After she appeared in recital at the Eaton Auditorium in Toronto in November of 1941, her career exploded.

In my most hopeful moments I imagine myself to be what Portia was—an artist. I fantasize about creating scenes as vivid and elegant as Watteau's *Fetes Galantes*. I ache to produce a single line that might echo the seductive whimsy of a Miles Davis riff. But I did not know these things about myself until long after my first encounter with Portia's life.

It was 1979 and I was a student at the University of Toronto, where one day I came face-to-face with a sepia-toned poster with the words "Ontario Black History Society" blazoned across the top. *Ontario...Black...History*. It never occurred to me that those words could be strung together just so. Not long after I called the organization to enlist as a volunteer.

Portia White was one of my first assignments. She had died more than a decade earlier, in 1968, and one of her sisters-in-law had offered to donate several boxes of the singer's papers to the OBHS archives. I arrived at Vivian White's cozy Scarborough bungalow on a sunny afternoon in spring. Mrs. White greeted me with a smile and led me into her kitchen where two medium-sized cardboard boxes sat on a large wooden table. The boxes were secured with tape, all ready to go. But I just couldn't wait to start. I began sifting through the material right there and then.

Those boxes contained more than one hundred clippings about Portia from all across the globe, some with excellent photographs attached. It was there that I first saw the 1941 picture of Portia standing amongst the festival contestants. There were dozens of itineraries and recital programs, many written in Spanish and all saved from Portia's 1946 Latin American tour. Vivian had generously contributed dozens of black-and-white photographs: several tiny 2x3's showing Portia aboard ship to somewhere in South America' some of Vinci alone and with his student; family shots; and, various publicity portraits ordered by her agents at Columbia Artists. Best of all by far were the handful of crinkly blue airmail letters. Each rustle of the tissue-like paper seemed to whisper a secret.

Although an increasing number of scholars are producing more detailed accounts of Portia's life, she remains a mysterious figure. No one seems to be able to say exactly why her career came to a sudden halt in the late 1940's, though a few years later in the mid-1950s she was diagnosed with cancer. Nevertheless, she gave one of her best concerts ever in 1955 at Trinity College in Toronto. After that she performed rarely. Instead, she coached a number of prominent entertainment figures including Dinah Christie, Lorne Greene and Robert Goulet. She died in February 1968. Thirty years after her death she is finally being recognized. [*Pride*, 2000]

Lady Sings the Blues

New York is calling Djanet Sears, the Canadian playwright whose *Harlem Duet* (1997), a contemporary urban blues rendition of Shakespeare's *Othello* played to packed houses at the Tarragon Extra Space in Toronto. A new larger production is currently underway at the Canadian Stage Theatre. On top of that, two theatres and one independent production house from New York are expressing interest. But Sears, who believes that "fate" is a mysterious force in life, is not ready to share any of the details. She's superstitious that way.

Take the Dora Mavor Moore Awards, for instance. *Harlem Duet* received several nominations in the small-theatre category. But Sears thought writing a speech ahead of time might jinx her chances. Big mistake. The play garnered a total of four awards: best new play, best production (Nightwood Theatre) and best director for Sears, while Alison Sealy-Smith won best female performance for her riveting portrayal of Othello's first wife Billie. A dazed Sears wound up at the podium three times with no prepared speech to fall back on.

"After awhile," Sears recalls gleefully, "I had no idea what I was saying. At one point I attempted to jot down some notes. But when I got on stage, I found I had only written the word 'Monday.'"

Sears breaks into a cascade of throaty laughter. Her excitement still hasn't abated. But then she really hasn't had time to reflect. For one thing she's been busy overseeing the changes to the new production. At the Tarragon, the set incorporated a cotton field that transports the audience back to the old South. The new stage lights up to reveal a room partly divided by a jagged crevice which, according to Sears, symbolizes "the manner in which history seeps up through the floors." Both sets were designed by Alan Booth, who has also reworked his haunting musical score for bass and cello.

Sears made the risky changes in spite of her general unwillingness to press her luck. "I wanted to give the actors a new challenge," she said. "To make it fresh for them...and for me."

With *Harlem Duet*, Sears gives us the prequel to *Othello*. "In Shakespeare's play Othello was in his 50s," Sears said, "I write about his youth, his life before he met Desdemona."

Sears's version is set in present-day Harlem where Othello (Nigel Shawn Williams), a university professor, makes a tortured decision to leave his wife Billie for a white co-worker named Mona. The action unfolds at the intersection of Lennox Avenue and 125th Street, better known as Malcolm X and Martin Luther King Blvds.

The location symbolizes the play's dynamics. At one level *Harlem Duet* explores the historical conflict about which ideology best sustains black emotional health: integration or separation. At another level, the play examines Billie's awkward, incorrect and painful feelings about the fact that the black man she adores is leaving her for a white woman.

It is a topic considered taboo for polite conversation. Even *Word*, Toronto's normally brash record of black culture, would only describe the plot in a curious urban double-speak: "The story begins when Billie discovers that her husband Othello, is leaving her for a colleague...and you know you sisters don't appreciate that!"

But Sears proves sympathetic to the dilemma of articulation. "On the one hand it's a marketing thing. You don't want to come across as though the play is heavy and political. It is primarily the story of a passionate love affair and the waning of a romance. It's written for everyone. At the same time, I'm not surprised that people have had a hard time finding the words to describe some of the emotions. The right words don't seem to be out there."

Lucky for us that Sears takes dramaturgy where plain speech fears to tread. *Harlem Duet* is a resonant medley of Shakespeare and the blues, two forms that share some important qualities, including a somewhat bawdy sense of humour. In *Harlem Duet* the desperate and delightful wit of Billie's landlord and best friend, Magi (Barbara Barnes Hopkins) keeps the laughter flowing. Still single and searching, Magi plans the date of her wedding and the birth of her child before either landing a husband or conceiving. Sears's blues also shares with Shakespeare the dramatic element of passion and betrayal (particularly the gut-wrenching scene where Othello admits desiring Mona's whiteness) and of course, madness, into which Billie descends, Lear-like.

"The experiences of black women are truly epic," said Sears, "because there are many levels to our stories. There's the human experience, the experience of one whom society may not view as equal, and then there is the experience of being a woman. And, of course, this is something Shakespeare does really well," Sears added, "many-layered stories."

Sears, her West Indian born parents and her three younger sisters, came to Canada from England when she was 15 years old. The family lived in Saskatchewan before settling in Oakville, Ontario.

The playwright's stately presence and braided coiffure may be familiar from the parts she's had in several television movies and Hollywood films, including co-starring with *NYPD Blue*'s Gail O'Grady in *Call for Help*. But Sears is perhaps best known for her 1989 one-woman show *Afrika Solo* which played in Toronto and Ottawa to critical acclaim. The story recounted her life-altering travels across Africa and was later adapted for radio.

Sears began working in earnest on *Harlem Duet* during her 1994-95 stint as writer-in-residence at Toronto's Nightwood Theatre. She went on to workshop the play at the prestigious Joseph Papp Public Theatre in New York, an institution renowned for its Shakespeare festival.

"I had never been to a theatre that big in my life," said Sears. "They have a casting department four or five people deep. It's huge. The people there set up three luncheons for me. They found me an apartment on Madison Avenue. I even had my own telephone line."

For Sears, the success of *Harlem Duet* has been like a dream. And what with the new production and New York calling and the fates smiling, it's one dream that won't be ending any time soon. [*Globe and Mail*, 1997]

Poetic Justice

At a recent book launch at the Barbadian Consulate in Toronto poet/novelist Dionne Brand could be seen darting through the crowd of animated literati with the unassuming sprightliness of a sparrow. At every turn peers, publishers and critics greeted the petite writer with great affection, embracing her and proffering congratulations on the publication of *Land to Light On* (1999), her most recent collection of poems.

It was a warm and fuzzy night. Still, many may find the concept of Brand, 44, as literary darling a little difficult to take. Not so long ago, a number of critics were busy excoriating the ardently socialist, lesbian feminist for views expressed in her collection of essays *Bread Out of Stone* (1994). Many of the pieces harshly indicted Canadian racism, along with patriarchal oppression and the world-wide legacy of imperialism. In response, a number of critics, some Trinidad-born like her, dismissed Brand with a string of durable signifiers: "the angry black," "the ungrateful immigrant," "the man-hating lesbian."

If the critical response was disappointing—the invective eclipsed discussion of the intensely lyrical quality of the essays—it was also somewhat surprising, since Brand's beliefs, at least in Toronto, were hardly unknown. *Bread Out of Stone* covered opinions previously articulated, though less prosaically, in books such as *Winter Epigrams* (1983), *Chronicles of the Hostile Sun* (1984) and her much discussed extended autobiographical poem *No Language is Neutral* (1990), the last shortlisted for the Governor-General's Award.

Practically from the moment of her arrival in Canada twenty-seven years ago, Brand has engaged in passionate polemic. She has been at the heart of Toronto's movement of black empowerment. A tireless activist, she has organized meetings, participated in demonstrations and involved herself in community programs to support black and immigrant women. She joined the Communist Party, and in 1983 left Canada for Grenada, eager to contribute to the island's socialist project.

"I needed to know that I was actually doing something; not just becoming co-opted and plugged into the big mass machine of Canadian state capitalism," she said in 1985.

Less than a year later with the US invasion of Grenada, she watched as the dream dissolved. While Brand survived, a number of her friends did not. A mournful Brand returned to Canada, where she applied her creative skills to film and literary projects centred upon recovering the histories of black Canadian women.

Brand possesses the manifestly un-Canadian desire to make the personal political. It is a stance that continually shapes her art. According to Nova Scotian poet and playwright George Elliott Clarke, Brand's perspective can easily be misinterpreted as sheer negativity. But Clarke situates her in a school that he calls "confrontational/confessionalism."

"Confessionalism is a type of poetry which can be pretty boring," Clarke said, "because the poet examines very personal autobiographical references that are frequently significant only to themselves. But Brand's poetry is confrontational confessionalism. She uses her life experiences to talk about oppression of many sorts in the Caribbean and in Canada. She attempts to find links between different kinds of oppression, and that is the strength of her work. It is multi-layered. There may be a nihilist tendency, but it is justified."

The ending of Brand's first novel *Another Place, Not Here* (1996), revealed her leanings toward nihilism. Nevertheless, it was received with enthusiasm. The response to *Land To Light On* has been similar.

Brand speculates about her growing acceptance. "I don't think my work has changed," she mused. "Maybe it is the reception of being published by a major publishing firm [M&S in poetry, Knopf for prose]. Or it could just be the politics of the times."

Carol Morrell, editor of *Grammar of Dissent* (1995), an anthology of the prose and poetry of Brand, Claire Harris and Marlene Nourbese Philip, believes Brand's stature is "more than a matter of literary fashion. There is a change in consciousness, an increased awareness among Canadian readers, that Anglo-American writing is not the only thing out there."

Morrell, an associate professor of English at the University of Saskatchewan, teaches Brand's poems and stories in her courses on Commonwealth and women's literatures. She describes Brand as part of a contemporary literary phenomenon. "Suddenly these voices are much more important. They are looking with fresh eyes at society. People can set the rhetoric of multiculturalism against the reality of racial prejudice."

Brand and I meet at the same coffee bar, near the same table where I interviewed her two years before. She appears decidedly less burdened, more easy-going, funnier even. She comes across as seeming a little less responsible for the world.

In fact, Brand admits to having reached a watershed moment. *Land To Light On* finds the poet trying to recover her political compass:

Look, let me be specific. I have been losing roads
and tracks and rivers and little thoughts
and smells and incidents and a sense of myself
and fights I used to be passionate about
and don't remember.

The book, Brand acknowledged, "started for me as I saw the (political) left being cut off at every corner by the powerful rise of corporate capital all over the world. I thought about the ability of huge corporations to influence governments to make laws that enable them to move their capital around more freely and reduce people's wages. And then I thought about the fight back against all of that that I would have been involved with. And how I and many other people were wondering what we were going to do next."

Land To Light On incorporates Brand's politics and poetics, each of which has always been in the service of the other. As she writes, in pointed reference to US poet Robert Frost, "I did not want to write poems about stacking cords of wood..."

Paradoxically, a good chunk of this collection proves as contemplative and romantically rustic as any Frost work, as well befits a poet living a solitary life in often snowy woods. A few years ago, Brand moved from Toronto to Burnt River north of Lindsay, Ontario where she inhabits a two-storey cabin on eight hectares of pine. Although she shares the dwelling, she spends extended periods alone, with only her books and her dog for company. Her days follow a soothing unvaried routine: she rises at 8 a.m. each day to put on the coffee and let out her dog, named for the blues singer Bessie Smith. Then she heads up to work in the second-floor office which has windows as large as doors.

"All I can see is snow and sky and pine," Brand said. "The nearest house is out of sight."

In an essay about Trinidad, "Just Rain, Bacolet," Brand describes the laboured progress of an ancient female leatherback turtle along a beach. The animal's massive shell attests to the length of time spent on Earth. I equate the image with Brand and her insistence on wearing her awareness of history upon her back, as it were. It is an attitude that defines her politics, art and her ordinary, everyday life. For example, the grandmother she often speaks of as though she were still alive, actually died more than thirty years ago. Her name was Amelia and she headed the bustling household in Guayguayare, Trinidad, where Brand grew up. The extended family consisted of Brand, her two sisters and a loud, loving assortment of cousins, uncles and aunts. For the children, their grandmother was "Mama." But they addressed everyone else, parents included, by their first names.

"She is present in my life," says Brand of the grandmother she adores. "If I have any quality of tenderness in me, it is from her."

After her grandmother's death, Brand's mother, Betty, returned from England, where she had been working as a nurse. "I didn't know my mother until I was 12. And we honestly didn't get along." Even today, she communicates little with the woman whom she rather coldly refers to as her biological mother. "It's just not a relationship I have."

Brand immigrated to Canada in her teens, living for a time with relatives in Sudbury. She came to Toronto a short time later. "I love this city like a 17 year old loves a place she goes to leave her family," she said with a laugh. One of the first things she did after her arrival was to abandon her straightened hairstyle in favour of a "big, big, Afro...It was such a symbol of joy." Later she joined a dance troupe led by renowned Toronto dancer Len Gibson. "It was an Afro, Cuban, jazz kind of mix," she recalled. Most significantly, she began writing for the black publication, *Spear*.

Today, living so far from "the clutter" of Toronto, as she calls it, Brand has less time for extra-curricular activities. She has also retreated from film production and her work gathering black Canadian histories. She pours all her energy into her own writing and seems content with that decision.

"It has always been a tussle with me between working in the community and writing," Brand says. "My political training says activism means activity. But I think I've resolved that over the last few years. My writing *is* my contribution, my offering to these political issues. And I see it as really important. Not more important, but as important, as calling a meeting." [*Globe and Mail*, 1997]

Phantom Hearts

Those evenings in Port-au-Prince. It was during the dictatorship of Jean-Claude Duvalier, and after dinner the electrical blackouts would begin. The old woman would seat herself on a chair in the courtyard. As soon as the children saw her they would gather about her feet. "Krik?" she called out when she was ready to start her story. "Krak?" they replied, when they were ready to listen. The children comprised a small crowd. Many, like 7-year old Edwidge Danticat, belonged to parents working abroad. This was the hour she treasured most. Soon the darkening sky would fill up with stars. In the twilight the black mountains that hovered over the sprawling quarter seemed to huddle nearer and the courtyard grew hushed. Though off in the distance, Edwidge could hear the clamour of the city; it was never completely quiet in Port-au-Prince. The old woman was the grandmother of Edwidge's aunt, and as she told her story, Edwidge and the other little girls took turns braiding her hair. The woman was known to hide small sums in the thick gray tresses and a lucky girl might loosen a coin that would be hers to keep.

Edwidge Danticat can never forget those long ago nights. The sound of the old woman's voice, the texture of her hair, and the sight of the flickering sky compose a precious tableau of her Haitian childhood. Some of the stories the grandmother told were folk tales Edwidge had heard many times and knew by heart, and some were stories about people in her own family. "Stay away from that pot!" the woman might say. "Your uncle drowned in a pot like that!"

"There was a great sense of justice," Danticat recalls. "Even though everything in life was so unbalanced, even though there was poverty and the dictatorship, in these stories all you needed to survive was a good heart, a good soul and good intentions."

By the age of 12, Danticat was living with her parents in New York, where storytelling still dominated the evening hours. Only the tales did not issue out of a lone voice into a dusky night, arriving instead via the television news.

There were reports from Haiti, where Jean-Claude Duvalier was attempting to crush opposition through a campaign of shocking violence. Thousands of Haitians were fleeing the island, mostly by boat. It seemed to Edwidge that every telecast opened with satellite pictures of her half-starved countrymen washed up on the shores of Miami. Next would flash images of Haitians peering bleakly through the bars of a detainment camp, that segued into a torrid account of a capsized dinghy. An update on escalating rates of HIV among the Haitian population might conclude the segment.

The news from Haiti sent a shudder through Danticat's family— through all of Brooklyn's expatriate island community. But it did not stir up much sympathy for Haitian students at Jackie Robinson Junior High where Edwidge and her friends were greeted each morning by the taunts of their peers. Schoolmates accused them of stinking of HBO (Haitian body odour) and of carrying the virus for AIDS. One day Edwidge's friend, fed up with the harrassment, threatened to place a hex over her tormentors. The American students weren't sure they believed in voudou, but the spell quieted them down for a while.

Edwidge lived in Flatbush with her father, a cab driver, her mother, a textile worker and her three younger brothers. At home they spoke Creole, but Edwidge spent every spare moment studying English. Haitian children were hounded mercilessly about their accents and she intended to lose hers fast. Soon Edwidge was speaking English so well she was invited to contribute to a local newspaper. She wrote a short essay about migrating to New York which became the seed for *Breath, Eyes, Memory* (1994).

Danticat's junior high peers should be feeling properly chagrined about now. The girl they taunted about her broken English has resurfaced as a modern-day master of the language. After *Breath, Eyes, Memory* appeared, the *New York Times Magazine* named Danticat one of thirty Americans under 30 destined to change the culture. The esteemed literary organ *Granta* crowned her one of the best twenty writers of the decade. *Breath, Eyes, Memory* is the story of Sophie Caco, who like Edwidge Danticat, migrates from Haiti to the US when she is 12. Sophie, like Danticat, feels lost and ambivalent upon reuniting with a mother she barely knows. The novel inverts some facts about the author's early life: where Danticat was cared for by her father's brother in the city, Sophie is cared for by her mother's sister in a village. Danticat has been careful to distance her own personal history from that of her heroine's. She describes the novel as containing much more emotional autobiography than factual occurrence.

Danticat spent her childhood in Port-au-Prince, yet like Haiti's oral storytellers, her novel celebrates village life. Her work resembles that of Haiti's "naïf" school of painters renowned for their depictions of peasant culture. Danticat's rural Haitian landscapes are streaked through with colour and studded with scenes of potluck meals and funeral processions, picturesque snapshots of communal life.

Breath, Eyes, Memory caught the attention of those with a sensitive cultural radar for exceptional literary talent. Danticat's second book did not disappoint. *Krik? Krak!* (1996) is a collection of stories about life in

Haiti set primarily during the Duvalier regime. It earned Danticat a nomination for the National Book Award and an introduction to a national audience. *Krik? Krak!* elucidates the experience of ordinary Haitians dwelling in an atmosphere of banal brutality. These stories display the author's matchless ability to portray a world she both despises and adores, a Haiti of idyllic beauty corrupted by unfathomable evil. A handful of the stories in *Krik? Krak!* were singled out for special merit. "A Wall of Fire Rising" describes a young poverty-stricken couple who nurture hopes for their son's future. "Between the Pool and the Gardenias" is a macabre, ironic vignette of a lonely woman who brings home a dead baby. But "Children of the Sea" emerged the undisputed favourite. It tells of a young political activist who escapes the country in a dilapidated boat packed with refugees. He writes to his girlfriend about life on the leaky vessel, although his letter may never be received. She writes too, about the increasing depravity of life in Port-au Prince. After reading "Children of the Sea" virtually every critic had this to say: "You will never look at boat people the same way again."

Nearly everyone who meets Edwidge Danticat comments that she seems wise beyond her years. One reason she gives this impression is that she looks years younger than she is. When I first met her in October of '98 she was 29 but might easily have passed for 16. Danticat is petite, with a flawless mahogany complexion and the kind of fresh, delicate features one associates with Italian cameos. Her gestures are likewise gracious and circumspect. It is hard to imagine her throwing her arms open wide with excitement or engaging in any sort of action that might take up more than her fair share of space. This sense of propriety extends even to the size of her books, the first two of which were published in compact form, as though Danticat wanted to make sure that plenty of room remained for other people's stories. It is this tacit regard for her neighbour that endows Danticat with a spiritual sagacity, the fact that she remembers to make room for people she can't even see.

Danticat's mien may be a natural consequence of her childhood in which she went about with a constant awareness of her absent parents. She did not remember her father, for he had migrated when she was a toddler. But she retained vivid recollections of her mother who left when Danticat was 4 years old. She was constantly being reassured that she would see her mother again, so that after a while her mother turned into a persistent, invisible presence.

Danticat's situation was completely ordinary among the Haitian youngsters she knew: "Like many children I grew up with, I was the child of migrant parents and was left with surrogates, my aunts and grandmothers and the grandmothers of other people. Some parents went to work in the United States or in Canada or in Guadeloupe. Some went to the Dominican Republic to cut cane. Although sometimes those that went to the Dominican Republic were never heard from again."

The separation of mother and child has been a prevalent theme in the lives of black women and a familiar refrain in their literature. In *The Autobiography of My Mother* by Jamaica Kincaid, the isolation of the motherless child dramatizes the psychological ravages of colonialism and the West Indian's alienation from Africa. In Toni Morrison's *Beloved* the relationship between mother and child is ruptured when a fugitive slave murders her baby daughter to spare the child the nightmare of bondage. Even the quintessential negro spiritual laments the separation of mother and child:

> Sometimes I feel like a motherless child,
> Sometimes I feel like a motherless child,
> Sometimes I feel like a motherless child,
> A long way from home.

"I felt this with my mother's absence," Danticat has said. "There were so many of us. And there are so many of us, whose mothers had to leave us—to separate from us—so they could give us a better life. It is the core of the migration story. You can't take everything with you."

In *Breath, Eyes, Memory* Sophie's mother Martine is a face in a picture, a disembodied voice on the recorded tapes she sends in lieu of written epistles to her unlettered relatives. Martine is a spirit that materializes after Sophie arrives in New York.

Mothers are not the only people cut off from loved ones in Danticat's work. Some people are imprisoned indefinitely, some flee in fear, some are beaten to death, some vanish walking down the street. Some die young from poverty and overwork and some, the lucky few, die perfectly natural deaths. This was not the bright future General Toussaint L'Overture envisioned for his countrymen when he led the insurrection that ended slavery in the French colonies in 1794. Haiti, the former Sainte Domingue, was the first country established by slave revolt. Danticat delights in dropping names of Haiti's revolutionary heroes. In *Breath, Eyes, Memory* there is the coal seller called Dessalines for the general who ousted the French forces in 1804; Sophie's surname, Caco, belongs to the guerrilla army that rebelled against America's occupation of Haiti during the early twentieth century. Martine's funeral at the end of the novel echoes the rhetoric of emancipation.

"Ou libere? Are you free my daughter," Grandmother Ife shouts as Martine's body is lowered into the ground.

"Ou libere," responds Martine's sister Atie.

Danticat sets *Breath, Eyes, Memory* and much of *Krik? Krak!* in the midst of the Duvalier years. "Children of the Sea" recreates the trauma of thousands who risk the six hundred mile voyage over open sea for a chance to live in America. The story also chronicles the hopelessness of those Haitians who remain at home.

An endless flow of untimely deaths invests Danticat's world with a ghostly magnetism, a spectral vantage that is not unique to Haitians. A number of Latin American writers—Gabriel Garcia Marquez and Isabel Allende—blend elements of the corporeal and the supernatural to depict their equally brutal culture.

Haitian writers turn to voudou (or voodoo) to explain the link between the living and the dead. Voudon's sacred cosmology, in which spirits reside in the physical world, forms the essence of Danticat's vision. Death for Danticat's characters is primarily a journey to join the ancestors. Many of the women live just long enough to pass down their stories to their daughters. Danticat suggests that knowing your mother's story is the same as absorbing her spirit. In this way ordinary Haitian women defy mortality.

A fortuitous dovetailing of events impelled Danticat's writing career: She migrated to America, she began to keep a journal, and she began to keep that journal in English. At school she plunged into her English lessons, not just because she was anxious to wash away all remnants of an accent, but because she was deeply curious to see how English worked. She toyed with it, was keen to learn how it might be manipulated to express her thoughts. Danticat is regularly applauded for the aplomb with which she navigates a second language but it is precisely because English is her second language that she maneuvers it so well. Danticat's particular facility with words earned her a full scholarship to Barnard where she studied French Literature and Economics. She spent her final semester in Paris translating *I, Tituba, Black Witch of Salem*, by Guadeloupan author Maryse Condé.

After graduation Danticat worked as a financial counsellor, and considered taking a post-graduate degree in economics. She contemplated studying nursing, as her parents would have liked. But the lure of literature proved too great. She was reading prodigiously by then: Haitians like Marie Chauvet and Jacques Romain, Americans like Toni Morrison and Paule Marshall, Alice Walker and Maya Angelou. These writers' books would powerfully influence her own. Although, if you ask Danticat the name of the storyteller she admires most she will almost certainly recall the old woman in Port-au-Prince.

"Those stories were my first creative writing lessons," she'll say. "From her I learned how to build suspense.... If the children grew bored

I saw how she would suddenly speed things up or insert a song. She was in tune with the listener. Her stories were tailor-made."

To no one's surprise Danticat did not take a post-graduate degree in economics but enrolled in the Master of Fine Arts program at Brown University. There she completed the manuscript for *Breath, Eyes, Memory*. It was published the following year.

In retrospect Danticat's literary success seems predestined. A precocious child, she was reading by age three. Her aunt was a street vendor and would bring Edwidge books. Edwidge especially loved Ludwig Bemelmans' stories about a little French girl. After reading about Madeleine in Paris, the 7-year old launched her own series about the adventures of Edwidge in Port-au-Prince. When she was nine, Danticat wrote a novel on plain white paper folded into tiny squares. The story, about a little girl visited at night by a group of female ancestors, eerily prefigured her future literary preoccupations.

As early as age 9, however, Danticat understood that Haitian writers were an endangered species. "While I was growing up most of the writers I knew were either in hiding, missing or dead," she wrote in a personal essay. "We were living under the brutal Duvalier dictatorships and silence was the law of the land. I learned that code of silence early on. It was as real as the earth beneath our feet, which was full of the blood of martyrs, among them many novelists, poets, journalists and playwrights who had criticized our government."

Dozens of Haitian writers fled to Quebec during the Duvaliers' reign, among them Gérard Étienne, Emile Ollivier and Dany Laferrière. Jean-Claude Duvalier went into exile in 1986. But in the following years the violence hardly slackened and it is doubtful that Danticat would have embarked upon a literary career had she remained in her native country. Once safely behind the American border, however, Danticat determined to pen the stories that, in Haiti, she would have never been able to write. Indeed, *Breath, Eyes, Memory* elicited outrage from many segments of the Haitian community. They felt that by exposing the shameful practice of testing—in which mothers test their daughter's virginity—she had betrayed her culture. The novel also describes the Duvalier regime with a subtle acumen that would surely have earned Danticat imprisonment or worse.

Danticat's third novel, *The Farming of Bones* (1998), chronicles a historical incident that has also received limited discussion in literary circles: the Dominican Republic's slaughter of thousands of migrant Haitian workers in 1937. Although the atrocity had not made its way into the history texts, Danticat had picked up bits and pieces of the story. The event struck her as too unwieldy for a novel. But one day she came across an article about a Haitian woman who had worked for a

Dominican family on a military base. The woman was serving dinner when Trujillo issued the order to kill and her employer got up from the table and stabbed her on the spot. Danticat knew she wanted to tell the story of the massacre from this woman's perspective; only in her version of the story the maid would live.

The Farming of Bones takes its title from the sound the cane makes when it is being harvested, a sharp crack like the snap of a chicken bone. The novel opens in the Dominican town of Alegria where Amabelle Desir, a maidservant in her early twenties, has spent most of her life attending to the needs of her employer Don Ignatius. Don Ignatius took Amabelle in when she was a child, after her parents had drowned in the Massacre River. As a Haitian, however, Amabelle remains an outsider. Her fiancé, Sebastien, a cane worker, explains, "Sometimes the people in the field when they are tired and angry say we are an orphaned people. They say we are the burnt crud at the bottom of the pot. They say some people don't belong anywhere and that's us."

Amabelle has enjoyed a warm relationship with Don Ignatius's daughter, but when the killing begins she bolts. Her journey back to Haiti is gruesome, littered with bodies. She arrives half-dead and has lost track of Sebastien. Amabelle's mother, father and lover disappear from her life without a trace.

"It's a kind of spiralling of losses which a lot of people I knew experienced," Danticat says. "There were a lot of people whose families did just disappear under the dictatorship, who remained the only one, or one of a few and there is something about it that gives one a great sense of determination, of wanting to survive and testify and not wanting to be forgotten."

After the massacre, offices are opened across the country so that people can relay their individual experiences for inclusion in the public record. When Amabelle sees the long line-up she considers ways of shortening her own tale. Anything, she thinks, that "would give a chance for someone else to be heard." There is a lot of Edwidge Danticat in Amabelle Desir.

Danticat writes the literature of survival, tinged with survivor's guilt. When relatives complain that she will not tell a happy story she says, "Maybe I'm not drawn to happy stories." Although Danticat may simply be displeased with the picture of Haiti being drawn as a modern-day, media-driven version of Conrad's "heart of darkness" because it discounts the experiences of ordinary, individual Haitians. In her story "A Wall of Fire Rising" a poor family walks to town each night to watch the state sponsored news on a public television in the village square. People linger long after the screen goes black, exchanging stories of their own.

With "A Wall of Fire Rising" Danticat notes that storytelling continues to play an invaluable role in communities that cannot depend on television (or radio, or film) to concern itself with their culture.

"I've always known from the depth of my soul that people have individual lives and individual beings. And that's what I want to write about. The political exists and it does affect the everyday, but we forget that people have dreams, that they love, that they hurt. That they must go from day to day, from hour to hour."

Which, of course, is the never-ending story. In Haiti, and everywhere else. [2001]

Digging Up a
Hidden Past

The most eagerly anticipated event of the autumn 1994 publishing season was the awarding of the inaugural Giller Prize. Businessman Jack Rabinovitch founded the prize in honour of his wife, the late Doris Giller, who was assistant Book Editor for the Toronto Star. Judges announced the winner at a black tie ceremony unrivalled in Canadian literary history for its glamour. The recipient was Kenyan-born M.G. Vassanji for *The Book of Secrets*, his epic tale set in East Africa.

Vassanji was one of two Indo-Canadians shortlisted for the lucrative $25,000 award. (Shyam Selvadurai was nominated for *Funny Boy*). Some critics felt moved to speculate on the recommendation of two minority writers, implying with a cynicism becoming reflex that such nominations were merely politically correct. Most critics, however, applauded evidence of a broadening canon, though overlooked for comment was the fact that Vassanji and a number of new Canadian writers speak to a quintessential Canadian experience. Whether the setting is Canada, as in his last novel *No New Land* (1991), or Africa, as in *The Book of Secrets*, Vassanji's exploration of how the past relates to the present describes a dilemma of deep interest to all Canadians.

Vassanji appears every bit the well-adapted new Canadian. He enjoys a comfortable lifestyle with his wife and two children in affluent North Toronto. Indeed, North America has brought him enormous success. After leaving Tanzania, where his family settled after his father's death, Vassanji studied at Boston's MIT and the University of Pennsylvania where he earned a Ph.D. in nuclear physics. He came to Ontario in 1978 to work for Atomic Canada and began writing in his spare time. He won the Commonwealth Writers Prize for best first novel in the African zone for his 1989 novel *The Gunny Sack*. His novel *No New Land* and his short story collection *Uhuru Street* (1991) won critical approval. Despite the approbation Vassanji admits ambivalence regarding his present life: "I am still attached to Dar es Salaam," he says of the Tanzanian capital he calls home. "Just the place, the ocean, the streets; the things that don't change."

His devotion to Tanzania largely explains the theme of preservation that pervades his work. In *The Book of Secrets* Fernandes, a retired history teacher, is given the diary of a colonial administrator named

Corbin. He attempts to recreate history by filling in the gaps in Corbin's personal account. But as Fernandes asks himself repeatedly, "Does anybody care about history?"

Vassanji himself bemoans what he calls a "thoughtless disregard for the past" among Indian communities. While he praises a persevering sense of community, he insists, "Something is lacking. We live in a world where dates matter."

Describing a recent trip to India he sounds positively indignant. "In New Delhi there's conscious acknowledgement of history. (But) all the buildings preserved there are the colonial buildings. It looks like Washington D.C., but there's all this other history. There's one of the most famous poets (Ghalib). India has made movies about him and everything. People can quote him. But I went to see the house where this poet lived and it was just rubble," he laughs ruefully. "Not even a house. And, of course, they spend millions of rupees making films [about him]."

Vassanji found that little recorded history of Indians in East Africa exists. *The Book of Secrets* is his attempt to reclaim some of this misplaced past. Like Fernandes, Vassanji hopes to fill in the gaps. But unlike many writers of colonized countries, Vassanji doesn't entirely blame the British for the erasure of Indian reports. Instead, his novel offers a recognition of the multiplicity of voices required to create a full picture.

Vassanji makes no effort to disguise his own limitations. For example, the story of the area's Swahili people remains largely untold. "Some things you don't know," he says, "and you have to be honest enough to admit it."

For Vassanji's characters, as for most real life immigrants, the past works as a touchstone, and memories of home, the assurance that one can go back, instills courage. Vassanji himself never consciously decided to leave Dar es Salaam for good. He describes himself as a student who departed for school and just never made it back. He frequently entertains thoughts of returning for good. Though, typically, he doubts he will: "A lot of it is cowardice. You see it as giving up a security."

Vassanji also stays for more positive reasons. "East Africa has some excellent schools; international schools. But the books they (assign) are not what I give my son to read. I asked them if they studied any African writers like the Nigerian writer Wole Soyinka. They said, 'No.' The curriculum is still European. It hasn't changed."

Ironically, one of the reasons Vassanji stays in Canada is to shield his son from a literary experience uniformly British. Even more ironic, that same British sensibility is what largely contributes to the popularity of his work. *The Books of Secrets* is stylistically reminiscent of Victorians like H. Rider Haggard. Yet Vassanji's writing also feels fresh and relevant. His characters continually look back to a severed past while trying to build a future. Their balancing act not only defines this country's condition, it identifies Vassanji as a writer profoundly Canadian. [*The Word*, 1994]

The Importance
of Being Different

In the lounge at Toronto's Royal York Hotel, Shauna Singh Baldwin is sipping a glass of Perrier and looking for all the world like the "sweet-sweet, good-good" Sikh woman at the centre of her novel *What The Body Remembers* (1999).

The book is set in the Punjab during the turbulent years leading up to the partition of India. It follows the heroine, Roop, as she is transformed from an inquisitive youngster into the unquestioning junior wife of a wealthy, polygamist landowner.

At 37, the Montreal-born Baldwin's perfect, heart-shaped face radiates a willingness to oblige. Her great eyes are fringed with heavy lashes that occasionally sweep down shyly against her cheeks. But her tongue is another matter. It can sometimes be as sharp as the *kirpan* the traditional Sikh warrior carried into battle. She is outspoken, sometimes cutting, especially when it comes to topics close to her heart, like cultural difference and the exclusion of people of colour.

Take the time she confronted Margaret Atwood about including only white Canadians in her stories. This was some years back when Atwood appeared before a capacity crowd in Baldwin's new home of Milwaukee. "I got up and said, 'Toronto is a multicultural city. I don't see how you can only write about European Canadians.'" Atwood coolly responded that perhaps people from other cultures should write their own stories. Thought Baldwin, "She's damn right!"

In other words, Atwood deserves at least part of the credit for the publication of this absorbing new novel. The story belongs to Roop, whose name means body or vessel, and Satya, whose name means truth. Sixteen-year-old Roop agrees to marry Sardarji, a wealthy engineer, because his first wife, Satya, has failed to provide him with children. Satya, who must endure the humiliation of being replaced in her husband's bed by a desirable girl, determines to make Roop miserable. As each of Roop's babies are born a malevolent Satya takes them for her own. Roop, as the junior wife, and a powerless woman in her husband's home, cannot object. The women look on as the world around them hurtles toward partition and the violence that will see the Sikh population decimated.

Baldwin recreates a vivid, pungent, tactile world full of the music of hymns and dirges, and clinking jewellery. *What The Body Remembers* may be the first novel to tell the story of the Partition from the view of Sikh women. There have been countless books on the partition of India from male perspectives and Muslim perspectives and Hindu perspectives and, of course, British perspectives.

"(But) look," says Baldwin, rolling her eyes in exasperation. "There have to have been Sikh women whose stories are interesting. Could I please hear about them instead?!"

In the relatively short period of time that Baldwin has been writing, she has enjoyed a good measure of success. Her first collection, *English Lessons and Other Stories*, was published in 1996 to unanimous praise. The stories, which are set between 1919 and 1991 are largely autobiographical and deal mostly with the complex inner lives of Indian women. In 1997, Baldwin received one of three $10,000 prizes from *Saturday Night* magazine for her story "Satya," which forms the basis for *What The Body Remembers*. Baldwin is new to the authors' circuit, but already specific themes are emerging. Her unwillingness to pander to anglophones is one motif. Though *What The Body Remembers* contains a plethora of Indian terms, Baldwin is adamant about not using a glossary: "I am a great proponent of the fact that you can read foreign literature without a glossary and be quite able to understand it.

"I was paid that compliment," says Baldwin, referring coyly to the absence of glossaries from British novels she read in India. "It was a compliment, wasn't it?" She arches an eyebrow like Vivien Leigh.

And no matter what questions one asks, Baldwin is likely to work her way round to her pet theme of racial, religious and gender differences. She makes no apologies for her preoccupations: "Difference is what causes problems. Difference caused the partition. For the people in my novel, the issue of difference is very important."

Of course, as a Sikh, Baldwin understands what it means to be perpetually perceived as different. Her grandparents were among the seventeen million refugees displaced by the division of India in 1947. Her parents moved to Montreal and Baldwin was born there in 1962. But the family moved back to Delhi when she was just seven years old. "It wasn't a good time to be a Sikh in Canada," she says.

In Delhi, Baldwin felt different again; this time like a Canadian, though that wasn't the only source of discomfort. "I wanted to fit in. I wanted to be dark. I wanted to be like every other Indian I saw. But we are Sikh. We're a minority in India, too."

Don't think Baldwin is complaining. She holds her heritage in high regard. She remembers how much of a comfort the Sikh faith was to her mother and grandmother. As a girl she thought there was nothing more beautiful in the world than the poetry of the ten gurus contained in the holy book. And although she describes herself as a moderate, Baldwin still visits the *gurdwara* (temple) regularly. She is a Singh, after all, and she wears her name with pride.

"The tenth guru said that all Sikh men should be long-haired and have the name Singh," she explains. "He said all the men should be lions and all the women princesses.

"It's the only religion in the world," she adds," in which the men and women are equal."

Still, in *What The Body Remembers*, as in real life, Sikhism falls far short of the principle of gender equality. Says Baldwin, "Some things are good and some things are not so good. I don't have to buy everything everyone says!"

These days Baldwin sees herself as belonging to three countries: Canada, India and the US. She is a Sikh in a largely Christian country and before that she was a Sikh in a predominantly Hindu land. She is a woman of colour in a white man's world. But what her body wants to remember is every aspect of her person. She refuses to push aside any element of her history. For years Baldwin asked herself, "How can I make my differences into something special?" In writing the lives of Sikh women, she has surely discovered her niche. [*National Post*, 2000]

Just Your Average Black Canadian Guy (Whatever That Is)

What it means to be a Negro in America can perhaps be suggested by an examination of the myths we perpetuate about him. —James Baldwin

A spoonful of sugar helps the medicine go down. —from *Mary Poppins*

In the late 1990s actor and playwright Andrew Moodie decided to stop doing American auditions. "I got tired of reading for Drug Dealer No. 1 and Drug Dealer No. 2," says the Ottawa native. "The last audition I did was for the 'university educated drug dealer' who had that speech about 'You have no idea what it's like on the streets.'

"All this crap defined by some white film producer in Hollywood or New York who has no idea about black culture in the first place. I got tired of participating in the stereotyping."

Luckily, Moodie does not have to rely on the whims of casting directors for his juicy roles; he can always create them for himself. What's more, he's very good at it. His first professional play, the 1995 comedy *Riot*, earned him a Chalmers Award. The story zeroes in on the lives of a handful of young black Canadians around the period of the 1992 Toronto riot.

Moodie's most recent play, *A Common Man's Guide to Loving Women* (1999), is currently running in Toronto. Amusing and insightful, the play is an inversion of the conventional motif in which a group of black women come together to disparage black men. Ntozake Shange first popularized the theme with her 1976 Broadway smash *For Colored Girls Who Have Considered Suicide*, and Terry McMillan has continued the tradition of excoriating black males in novels such as *Waiting to Exhale*.

In *A Common Man's Guide*, however, it is the women who dog the men; the men are hapless doggees. The play opens during a stag for Chris (Derwin Jordan), a lawyer whose fiancée has just called to cancel the wedding. Wendle (Conrad Coates), the director of finance for a marketing firm, has his own problems: his girlfriend has just charged him with rape and he is in danger of losing his job. Even the jocular

Greg (Andrew Jason Wade) suffers romantic delusions, as the woman he hopes to engage in a serious relationship desires a mere sexual fling. Moodie has given himself the role of Robin, a happily married man harbouring a distressing secret.

It is an evening of camaraderie and commiseration that includes a playful and profane consideration of the age-old stereotypes about black men, their women and interracial relationships. An evening, in other words, with four of your average black Canadian guys.

"I think that to a large degree what we see about black men is defined by American culture. We as Canadians inherit that," Moodie explains.

"But I want to show us as we are, to be able to take a snapshot, or to use a close zoom-in camera, so that we are watching the lives of black Canadians. I want the characters to be oblivious to the fact that we are observing them so that we can see how their colour and culture weave in and out of their lives."

Several lifetimes ago, before he was an actor or playwright, and while still a student at Fisher Park High in Ottawa, Andrew Moodie, a first-generation Jamaican Canadian, was an angry black man.

"I went through this phase," Moodie recalls. "I was reading (Black Panther) Bobby Seales. *Seize the day! The white male industrial complex must die! I will fight with my brothers! Fight the power!!!*"

We are sitting at a long table in the boardroom at the Canadian Stage Company in Toronto, and Moodie is gesturing ludicrously, mimicking his younger idealistic self and parroting the bywords of the militant sixties. He is sporting a bomber jacket and, with his low afro and wide, expressive eyes, he still looks young enough to be in high school. Nevertheless, the image of Moodie as a railing teenaged radical is not one that surfaces easily. It clashes with his funny, straightforward, yet somehow measured responses, his ultra-Canadian guardedness.

Equally incongruous is the idea of any sort of African sensibility flourishing in the midst of Ottawa's cool conformity. Moodie himself admits that the notion of a true black Canadian identity has yet to take hold.

"It's a tricky thing in Canada," he says. "Canada is built on the concept of group rights. The moment you say you are a group, you have to define yourself. People want to know: do you need special rights like a native person? Or do you want to be distinct like a Quebec person?"

Moodie delved into the topic of group rights in his play *Oui* (1998), a story about a Franco-Ontario family divided over the Quebec referendum. Interestingly enough, in *A Common Man's Guide to Loving Women* one of the crucial distinctions Moodie makes between black Canadian culture and African-American culture is language.

Early on, Greg advises the newly single Chris on how to flatter an American woman: "Just say Mmm mm *mmm!* Get a look at yourself! Girl you looking so good right now, I would sop you up with a biscuit!" Robin concurs: "Americans love that shit!"

The vernacular might be different, but the stereotypes are the same. In conversation, Moodie, like a number of black Canadian male artists, including novelist Andre Alexis and poet George Eliot Clarke, generally de-emphasizes the significance of race, but his characters are often as bold and brazen as he himself is cautious. In *A Common Man's Guide* he tosses sensitive racial stereotypes into the dialogue like so many hand grenades, while audience members sit with bated breath waiting for them to explode. When Chris's fiancée leaves him, for example, his friends encourage him to take up with a white woman because they are easier to please than black women.

And the four friends continuously refer to the superior endowments of black men. The condom has not been made that will suffice. It's all very tongue-in-cheek, but it still feels dangerous.

Says Moodie, "When I first had the idea of doing this play, (I wanted) to have black men on-stage speaking honestly. (But) you have to have a certain context. As black men we joke around in a very ironical fashion. The statements we make are actually the opposite of what we seem to be saying."

Moodie's playfulness with black stereotypes exemplifies a tradition in which black men embrace negative images as a means of exerting control over them. Writing such provocative dialogue often requires that Moodie walk a fine line between verisimilitude and offensiveness. He uses his sense of humour to defuse tension. "If you're entertaining, and you keep on being entertaining, audiences are pretty open—you can reveal so much about your culture."

In *A Common Man's Guide*, Moodie seems more interested in exploring stereotypes than exploding them. Especially when it comes to stereotypes about black men and their treatment of women. Wendle is devastated that his girlfriend, who is white, has not only accused him of rape, but has also evoked the spectre of O.J. Simpson. In Moodie's Canadian take on the dilemma, however, race does not trump gender.

"For years now we black men have been saying, 'We are human beings. You respect us. I know why you're not hiring me. I know why you're not giving me this apartment.' And now we have to be able to turn around and say to women, 'We must respect you as human beings as well. And you have absolute and complete control over your bodies.'

"Black men don't always respect women. Sometimes they take the pain that has been forced on them by society and they vent it toward women, especially black women. The men in this play are savvy, but they are just as capable of being victims (of these attitudes) as well."

Moodie overcame his racial angst by devouring the works of black writers such as James Baldwin, Richard Wright and the Jamaican Pan-Africanist Marcus Garvey.

"I read and read and read until I got this bedrock sense of myself, so that (now) I can be comfortable with my skin colour and my culture and my people and my gender."

Still all this consciousness-building has not prevented Moodie from clinging doggedly to one gratifying myth: that of the well-endowed black male. "The penile size thing," he says with a cheeky grin. "That's a stereotype black men hold on to with every fibre of their being." [*National Post*, 1999]

The We of Blackness

If there is anything that disturbs Hilton Als, it is the tragedy of the life unlived. With his new memoir *The Women* (1998) Als takes his place within a long tradition of black authors whose works consider the dream deferred. Yet Als is one of the few black American authors who balks at the suggestion that his writing can be defined by race; if there is anything Als disdains, it is the "we" of blackness.

"I don't really believe in the construction of 'we,'" said Als, who was in Toronto recently to read at the festival celebrating African identity. "When you talk about your experience, you can't imagine, or know, what it feels like to be another person. You can't ascribe motives to other people."

It seems ironic then, that Als, who will be 36 next month, devotes the greater part of his energies to writing intimate and searching profiles. The biographical essays that make up *The Women*, for example, attempt to sort through the labyrinth of emotions that propelled three intriguing figures, all of whom lived unfulfilled lives: the author's Barbadian-born mother, Marie, whom he idolized and emulated; his mentor and lover, poet Owen Dodson (popular among black Americans in the 1940s and '50s); and Dorothy Dean, a Harvard-educated black woman, who in the 1960s became the social arbiter for an elite clique of gay white males.

"What I do is research what [my subjects] did and then I describe what they did," Als said over dinner at a Thai restaurant. "It's through the description that the motivation shows itself. I don't really say that they are this or they are that."

Als, who writes for the *New Yorker*, is a bear of a man, round and broad, more teddy than grizzly. But he is tough in his determination to free himself from what he believes is the trap of racial identification. In his essay on Dodson, Als dismisses the esthetic of the "new negro" that emerged during the Harlem renaissance of the 1920s and '30s. He faults black American literary icons of the period, including Alain Locke and Langston Hughes, for focusing on black ideology rather than more existential concerns. According to Als, they set a faulty precedent that continues to influence the vast majority of today's black writers.

"In the modern world," Als said, "one of the ways black people can be more interesting is to believe in themselves, and to marry themselves, as opposed to marrying this abstraction known as race."

Like Dodson, Als is "female-identified." (He sometimes calls himself an auntie-man, the colloquialism for homosexuals in Barbados, and also frequently refers to himself as a "negress.") Als expresses the same impatience with the correctness of contemporary gay politics as he does with the movement for black empowerment. Though he appears to find homosexual a less restrictive category than black.

On the whole, however, he is unconcerned about his place in the scheme of things.

"I'm not really interested in the scientific reasons for who I am and why. I don't know anything about the way I was born or not born. I think that in my conscious life I've made the best of what I have. I don't know where I got what I have, but I made my peace with it a long time ago."

Als was born and grew up in Flatbush, Brooklyn. The area at the time was largely Jewish, and Als, his mother, an older sister and a younger brother occupied the upstairs flat of a brownstone. "Flatbush was very small and...strangely neighbourly. You knew everyone," he said.

He attended Intermediate Public School 320, but would sometimes cut class to spend the day in the biography section of the local library. He remembers reading about the lives of Clara Barton and Eleanor Roosevelt.

"I was really the worst truant," he said, "because they would never find me in the park smoking dope. I was always in the library reading. I mean, what could they say?"

Around age 13, Als took to wearing a silk ascot to school in the style of nineteenth century journalist Horace Greeley. His English teacher called him "a little esthete," and fed his intellect with a steady supply of books. An insomniac, Als began writing stories at night to keep himself company, but for years he wrote in secret.

His mother shared his love of reading, introducing him to her own favourite books, including Paule Marshall's *Brown Girl, Brownstones*. He was also very close to a sister who was eleven years his senior. They spent hours in her room dancing to Dionne Warwick's "Don't Make Me Over." He would help her get ready for dates.

In *The Women*, Als chronicles these early years with spare and articulate grace. He possesses that rare ability to write honestly of intimate experiences without degrading himself or anyone else. Even while he seduces us into his story, he remains cool and distant. Als is an enigmatic presence, on and off the page.

"Well, of course," he said, "it's an artist's prerogative: You have to learn how to withhold. The saddest thing about the culture at large right now is that mystery has become synonymous with confusion. No one wants to accept the fact that there is a lot of mystery in the world." [*Globe and Mail*, 1997]

A Quality of Light

Novelist Richard Wagamese believes in magic: "Magic is part and parcel of everyday life. People call it faith, coincidence, kismet. But it's always there," says the Ojibway author of *A Quality of Light* (1997). One classic example came just before a recent Blue Jays game at SkyDome in Toronto. Wagamese was watching batting practice and wishing he could take home a ball for his toddler son. Suddenly, "Carlos Delgado hits a practice pitch and it lands right in my hands," recalls Wagamese, still excited. "I'm like, 460 yards away, and it lands right in my hands. Now that's magic," he says, "'cause I wished it."

A mystical *Field of Dreams* atmosphere illuminates *A Quality of Light*. In the novel, baseball serves as the foundation for an enduring friendship between two pre-adolescent boys—one native, one white. Joshua Kane, the story's narrator, is a native boy adopted at birth by a white farm couple who raise him with great love and staunch Presbyterian values. His friend Johnny Gebhardt wishes he were native, so that he might replace his own brutally dysfunctional family history with one he deems more heroic. When classmates ridicule Josh and Johnny for their poor baseball skills, the pair make a secret pact to become the school's best players.

This early section of the novel may seem like a plot lifted from a Disney film, but Wagamese bases the events on the most significant achievement of his largely unhappy childhood. Born in 1955, Wagamese spent his earliest years on the Dalles Reserve near Kenora in northwestern Ontario. He and his extended family lived a traditional lifestyle in the bush, trapping, hunting and fishing. Family difficulties eventually forced Wagamese and his siblings into foster care. A southern Ontario family adopted Wagamese when he was nine. Unfortunately, the relationship failed miserably. It was, as he succinctly puts it: "Trauma from Day One."

Wagamese speaks passionately and laughs often. He enjoys relaying the amusing anecdote. But talk about his adoption makes him wary. Painful memories quickly surge to the surface. "I came out of Northern Ontario where there was nothing but trees and rocks and lakes," Wagamese explains, "and suddenly, I'm in the middle of the Holland Marsh where there are scrawny trees and brown water. It was like Mars to me; like being on a whole new planet. There was nothing to help me make a transition. It was like, 'This is your home now. Get used to it.'"

On the first day at his new school the kids teased him about his ignorance of baseball. So, like Josh and Johnny, he set out to master the game. Wagamese headed to the library for some information, "I remember the librarian found me a picture book about the rules...plus another book that had all the measurements." At home he painted a strike zone on the back of an old sheep shed and practiced every free moment he had.

That was the first time he discovered the transforming power of books. "Books saved my life," he says. Wagamese ran away from his adoptive family a couple of times. At 16 he left their home for good. With nowhere to go, he turned to the streets of St. Catharines, where he kept company with a band of bikers and drug dealers.

Every once in a while, though, he would feel the need to escape. Sometimes he would take a bus to Toronto. He would hunker down at the back of the Parliament branch of the public library and lose himself in a book for days at a time. "I read a lot of trash," he says. "But I also found out what I liked. I read some Ayn Rand, Nevil Shute and Michael Ondaatje." He also enjoyed the classics, *A Tale of Two Cities* and *War and Peace*.

Wagamese's street life led to problems with alcohol and drugs and eventually landed him in jail. But in one of those magic twists he loves to point out, incarceration enabled his brother to track him down. The reunion started Wagamese on a protracted journey to reconnect with his Ojibwa heritage.

Wagamese, who has worked as a disc jockey, a newscaster and a columnist for the *Calgary Herald*, incorporates much of his traditional culture into his fictional technique. His kinetic use of language is one example: "Aboriginal language is verb-based as opposed to English which is noun-based. So, for example, there is no such thing as a tree, 'but a tree that blows softly in the wind.'"

Wagamese also sees his facility with language as providing a suitable response to writers such as W.P. Kinsella, whom he accuses of depicting aboriginal people as "guttural, slow-thinking and basically illiterate."

Still, he can't help but admire Kinsella's baseball stories, particularly "The Thrill of the Grass." "It's the most amazing story," he says, "because it's about taking the grass back into the stadium.

"After all," he continues, laughing, "I don't think you can get as much of a sense of baseball from carpet burn as you can from grass stains."

Aboriginal traditions also influence Wagamese thematically. In *A Quality of Light*, Josh and Johnny embody the two most common approaches to reclaiming aboriginal identity. Joshua's profound spirituality and his exploration of native rituals lead him to gain a sense of his heritage. Johnny, who fancies himself a warrior, believes natives must seek political, even violent solutions, in order to recover their stolen heritage.

Joshua's peaceful conciliatory narrative personifies Wagamese's own belief that aboriginal communities need to emphasize spiritual healing.

"The wellness in communities has to be given equal importance to the political process," he says. "Everyone is really pressing for a political solution [to native problems]. They want to revisit the constitutional process; they want to look at amendments to the Indian Act; they want to implement changes to the Royal Commission. But it's an aboriginal maxim that nothing in the universe ever grew from the outside in."

Wagamese now realizes that his own spiritual healing began the year he turned nine and encountered the magic of baseball. "Every February I say to my friends that the world is about to become real again, especially when pitchers and catchers report for spring training. Baseball is my ultimate connection to my childhood. It's the most magical thing that happened to me as a kid—and the one love affair I've had all my life." [*Globe and Mail*, 1997]

Consecrated Ground

Driving north from Halifax along Barrington Road. To the west the land slopes upward and is cluttered with prefabricated houses. To the east, a rolling expanse of manicured lawn hugs Halifax Harbour. Seaview Park they call it now, though for two hundred years it was the site of Africville, one of the oldest free-standing black communities in North America. The black loyalists who settled here in the late 1700s possessed land grants from the crown.

Others—and much has been made of this—erected domiciles without permission. Over decades, rural blacks migrated to Halifax in search of work; many of them quickly constructed houses in Africville and the area took on a makeshift appearance. But it was home. The people built a school. (The contralto Portia White taught there in the 1930s). And they built a place of worship. The community's throbbing heart was the Seaview Baptist Church. The area had its local heroes as well, including world renowned boxer, George Dixon.

To outsiders, though, Africville was an eyesore, a shantytown and worse, a "ghetto." Halifax officials did what they could to dissuade development. They refused to install running water or sewage systems. They offered nothing in the way of municipal services (although a dump for city garbage was eventually opened). Still, the people would not be moved. Indeed, they grew willful in their tenacity and self-reliance, so that in the end the politicians felt they had no option. Africville was slated for demolition.

Between the early '60s and mid-70s the residents were relocated to nearby public housing projects. In time, every building in Africville was razed to the ground, including the Seaview Baptist Church, which disappeared in the dead of night.

Nova Scotian playwright George Boyd dramatizes the demise of Africville in his play, *Consecrated Ground* (2000), which he brings to Toronto as part of the AfriCanadian Playwright Festival's series of staged readings. Boyd, who was born in 1952, did not grow up in Africville, but on nearby Creighton Street in the north end of Halifax.

Still, he remembers friends of his parents gathering in the living room to discuss their outrage over the dilemma. Says Boyd: "I remember the expression on their faces."

Consecrated Ground is the former Newsworld sportscaster's most recent work. He has also written *Shine Boy* (1988) the story of George Dixon (who held the world featherweight title throughout the 1890s);

and *Gideon's Blues* (1989) about the devastating impact of crack cocaine on Halifax's black community. *Gideon's Blues* was based on his award-winning documentary on the topic. And he has co-authored a radio play, *House of Flowers* (1997).

Consecrated Ground tells the story of an Africville couple, Clarice and Willem, whose baby is bitten by a rat from the city dump. When the play opens, the bulldozing has already begun. But Clarice insists on staying put. What's more, she intends to bury her dead child in the place where generations of her family have lived. But the social worker denies her request, since as far as the city is concerned, Africville has no consecrated ground.

It was the title that came to Boyd first. "I kept having a picture in my mind of the church being razed, which is an image of desecration. And really, it's not often you see a church torn down. It gives you a creepy feeling." The image is especially disturbing to black Nova Scotians, for whom the church remains a central fact of life.

"The figures of Clarice and her baby represent Africville and its people," Boyd continues. "I see the community as a mother. It has to be fertile and reproduce in order for it to survive."

Boyd is not the only Canadian to immortalize the event. Joe Sealy has written the Juno Award winning *Africville Suite* (which will serve as musical accompaniment to the Toronto reading); Faith Nolan has celebrated the area in her folk songs; Maxine Tynes, Charles Saunders, George Elliott Clarke and others have written elegies and poems.

The story resonates for black Nova Scotians whose presence in the area goes back nearly three hundred years. For them, Africville represents a place of belonging in a province with a racial history akin to that of the Jim Crow South. But how will *Consecrated Ground* be received in Toronto, where black people increasingly reject depictions of the unpleasant past?

"What I would say to those people," says Boyd, "is that I'm not going to raze my memory the way they razed Africville. I don't believe that my history is any less rich or beautiful or compelling than anyone else's history."

Besides, he adds, "If you're an artist you ought to be prepared to tell the truth. To my way of thinking truth can be enlightening, it really can set you free—and move you on down the road." [*National Post*, 2000]

Race, Film and History

The other night at the University Center for the Arts in Buffalo the documentary filmmaker Ken Burns addressed a capacity crowd on the art of biography. Burns is frequently described as the pre-eminent documentary filmmaker of his generation. His epic all-American works—including *The Civil War* (1990), *Baseball* (1994) and *Jazz* (2001)—appear regularly on PBS, and often examine their subjects through the prism of race. That night, Burns led his audience on a spirited tour through the complex personalities featured in his American Lives Series: *Thomas Jefferson*, *Frank Lloyd Wright* and *Mark Twain* to name a few. As engrossing as what Burns said was how he said it. His fluid, lyrical delivery was every bit as mesmerizing as that of the bewitching storytellers who narrate his films.

What distinguishes Burns's documentaries, however, is not merely the quality of voice, but the quantity; what he likes to call his chorus. He takes pains to incorporate a vast number of varied American viewpoints, academic and popular, northern and southern, male and female and, most significantly, black and white. In *Mark Twain*, for instance, the sonorous tones of African-American narrator Keith David strike a counterpoint to the lilting southern cadences of Kevin Conway's Twain. Similarly, the expertise of African-American scholar Jocelyn Chadwick and the white historian Ron Powers combine to produce a fresh, integrated vision of *The Adventures of Huckleberry Finn*, Twain's racially-contentious masterpiece. Burns himself admits he is on a mission to integrate the various strands of the American story; to make America's separate black and white histories into one.

"It's really important to me to have a variety of perspectives," Burns says in an interview earlier that day. "And if you do that then it's an inclusive story. The Civil War was not just about Lincoln and Ulysses S. Grant and Robert E. Lee. It was about ordinary soldiers and African-Americans who were active, dedicated and self-sacrificing warriors in an intensely personal drama of self-liberation.... I think that when you literally integrate perspectives of your storytelling, the result is much more complicated, [there's a] great deal of undertow. It also allows for this sense of oneness of identity."

Burns, who is divorced and the father of two daughters, was born in Brooklyn, New York in 1953. He was raised in Delaware and Michigan and now resides in the small, "lily-white" town of Walpole, New Hampshire, which is home to his production house Florentine Films. His first documentary for Public Television, a history of the Brooklyn Bridge, aired in 1982. Since then he has produced nearly two dozen award-winning films for PBS including in-depth profiles of the region-alist painter Thomas Hart Benton (1989) and architect Frank Lloyd Wright (1998). His upcoming film, *Horatio's Drive*, about the first cross-country journey by automobile, is scheduled for broadcast in fall of 2003.

Burns's story is not always race, but it is always America. He believes that the theme of slavery, and the subsequent struggles of black people, cannot be neatly excised from the main plot. This is partly because the motif of race has worked itself deep into his own life story. Burns's mother died of breast cancer when he was eleven and her slow, traumatic passing is inextricably linked in his mind to the worst violence of the civil rights era. "I remember as a little boy that I transferred a lot of anxiety about my mother's impending death to the civil rights move-ment," Burns recalls. "When I saw [on television] dogs and firehoses unleashed on demonstrators in the South, it tortured me. Maybe I tried to avoid the cancer that was killing my mother by transferring my focus to the cancer that was killing my country."

His recently deceased father, a professor of anthropology, exerted his own influence. Burns often refers to himself as "passionately committed to excavating the story of race." He defines this practice as "emotional archaeology."

In any honest retelling of American history, says Burns, the issue of race is present naturally. *Not For Ourselves Alone* (1999), Burns's portrait of suffragists Elizabeth Cady Stanton and Susan B. Anthony, features segments examining the politics that exacerbated dissension between black and white women. In *Thomas Jefferson* he studies the obvious contradictions in the slaveholding president's perceptions of liberty.

The filmmaker's ten-year plan includes a profile of America's first African-American heavyweight champion Jack Johnson, and he is currently engaged in talks with the family of Martin Luther King, Jr. So far it is Burns's acclaimed trilogy—*The Civil War*, *Baseball* and *Jazz*—that comprises his most thorough and eloquent consideration of the way slavery has sculpted American history. "I'm interested in a true, honest, complicated past," Burns says.

Still, he is not completely sanguine. At one point during our interview his soft, lullaby voice goes sad and strange: "I get a lot of hate mail," he says, glancing nervously over his shoulder. "Maybe using 'a lot' is not a good description," he quickly retracts. "It's probably less than one percent."

What bothers him more, he says, is the veiled racism he encounters in friends and acquaintances, which communicates itself as impatience. "People ask: 'Why do you keep bringing up the story of blacks. Why'd you make Jackie Robinson and the Negro leagues the focus of *Baseball*?' Well, to me baseball wasn't very interesting except that it was a vehicle to continue to talk about race."

Burns also received sharp criticism for omitting important white musicians from his ten-episode, seventeen and a half hour ode to Jazz: "I felt if I was making a film on the greatest painters in the world I'd have to admit that there are no African-American painters in my top ten. But if you're talking about jazz musicians, the top ten are all African-Americans. I'm unapologetic about that," he says.

Indeed, it may be a mistake to view Burns as a blazing altruist, advocating on behalf of African-Americans. Rather he is an accomplished artist, unwilling to compromise his oeuvre, his ever-evolving biography of the American nation. When race bubbles to the surface of Burns's work it is only because he sees it as "the burning centre of the American story."

"It's not just the question of race," he explains, "but the whole question of singing the epic verses of my country. And I'm determined to sing them as loud as I can." [April, 2002]

Interviews

Toni Morrison:
War and Peace

Ivisited Toni Morrison in the winter of 1998 on a grey day in Manhattan, just after the publication of her novel *Paradise*. Toni Morrison is the first American since Faulkner to receive the Nobel Prize for Literature. She won a Pulitzer in 1987 for her stunning portrayal of slave history in the novel *Beloved*. Born in Lorain, Ohio, in 1931, Morrison is widely regarded as America's greatest living novelist. Her first novel *The Bluest Eye* was published in 1970. Since then she has written eight novels altogether, including *Sula* (1973) and *Song of Solomon* (1977) which recreate for African-Americans their hidden past. Her next novel *Love*, will appear in fall of 2003. Morrison has written a book of literary theory: *Playing in the Dark: Whiteness and the Literary Imagination* and has published a number of books on racism in America including *Race-ing Injustice, En-gendering Power* (1992). We met at her elegant loft. I remember being struck by how beautiful she was and by her large almond-shaped eyes which disconcertingly sized me up. We sat at the kitchen table and she served coffee. We spoke for about an hour and a half, with the phone occasionally interrupting. Afterward, she offered to take me to lunch. The restaurant was a few blocks from her building. I'll never forget the way everyone just froze when she walked into the room.

Donna Bailey Nurse: *Paradise* feels like one of those sweeping, old-fashioned sagas, too large to fit between the covers of a book.

Toni Morrison: I thought this book was the longest book I'd ever written. It was five hundred and thirty pages. And it kept getting longer and longer. Of course I doubled and tripled spaced and made big type so I could see it when I put it on the computer. But in the end it was two hundred pages shorter than I thought it was.

DBN: I am so curious to know: Did we really have this past you write about in *Paradise*—ex-slaves wandering the country in homeless bands, starving, and then some, eventually, founding all black towns. Is this a history that is already available to the reader or are you just piecing it together as you go along?

TM: Some of it I knew about but not in depth. My parents were what they used to call "race people" who used to be on top of every issue, every law [that] passed, every moment of progress, every retreat. They read the black press and J.A. Rogers. However, I wasn't terribly interested in all that growing up. I was very much interested in what was going on in the school system, reading American literature, classical literature, what have you. I was a very avid reader. So I got sort of a limited education as far as black history was concerned, in spite of the fact that my parents were intense about it. But like any young person (I told myself) that I am going to know better and more than they. Until I left Ohio, which is where I was living, and went to Howard University which is a predominantly black college. Howard was a deliberate choice on my part, because I really wanted to be with smart black people.

I came about black history in depth as an undergraduate. But there were certain areas that were still unknown to me: one was Reconstruction. Most of what we hear about Reconstruction was that it was all terrible. But in fact it was a powerful, extraordinary eight or ten years. And the fact that following it was this Klan movement was testimony to its success. When blacks get truly powerful, whites always get nervous. The enormous success of blacks during Reconstruction is the reason the period has been distorted and played down in history.

On the other hand, I knew a little history about the foundation of black towns because I taught in Texas when I just got out of graduate school. But I thought they were like college towns: places like Langston, Oklahoma. What I didn't know until later was how many all black towns there were and how long they lasted. And they were not shack towns. They were towns full of schools and banks and stores and mills and so on.

The founding of all black towns was a very powerful movement. Some of the towns are still there. Recently I read in the *Wall Street Journal* about a town called Taft, Oklahoma and I did a little hiccup because it was founded the same time Haven in *Paradise* was founded and it had four hundred people in it. They were hoping to get funding to have the town made into a landmark. And that was amazing to me. There's a world of history out there.

DBN: One of my favourite historians is Nell Irvin Painter. She writes marvellously about obscured black history.

TM: Yes. She's one of the historians bringing attention to that era. But again, it's in the academy. I'm always disturbed that in the public discourse you are always hearing about how black people ought to take care of themselves. And yet there has always been this historical pressure in the community to make our own way and not ask anybody for anything. Ever.

DBN: Part of what struck me was how the women in Ruby were eager to send their sons away to the army. It was almost as though they believed war was safer for their black sons than the civilian world.

TM: People don't talk about it. But black children were sent in to the army because it was a protected environment. It was safer.

DBN: It's this odd irony, because black people are always depicted as the most violent people.

TM: We've been demonized and criminalized, when really we were the ones running from and trying to protect ourselves from violence. When I was young we used to run from white boys. That was the norm.

DBN: I had to run from white boys too.

TM: We were trained to avoid those people. But it's my sons who are stigmatized.

[We are interrupted by a phone call by a friend who wants to talk about Michiko Kakutani's harsh review of *Paradise* in the *New York Times*. She is laughing a lot, although the laughter is quite wry.]

DBN: I am surprised that at this point in your career you are particularly interested in what critics might have to say about your work.

TM: I don't care about these things in relation to my work...at all. I do care about the way in which African-American fiction is perceived, reviewed, handled and understood. I teach it. I have tracked it over time from the days when it was patronized to the days when it was treated purely as sociology to these days in which it is taken seriously. I watch and care quite a bit.

I have a dual role. Like a representative role. I have seen the days in which Maya Angelou and Alice Walker, Toni Cade Bambara or Gayl Jones and myself, were reviewed abominably, in terms which were inapplicable. And I've seen that change in the scholarship, so that when I read reviews of my own work it doesn't have any effect on my work, how I write or what I am going to write, or how I think about writing...at all. I am very...cold about the relationship between reviewers and work.

Very cold. I have no expectations. It is very interesting to me, mostly because it is so revelatory about the reviewer.

But I care very much that the body of work that black people do in this country is understood to be significant, important, varied. I remember days when I was reviewed along with James Alan Macpherson, and Gayl Jones in a book review. The reviewer tried to pull it all together when the work was incomparable. We have nothing in common except the colour of our skin. And the reviewer had the nerve to decide which of the three books were better. She may have been right. But the reason she said that James Alan Macpherson's was better was because his view of black life was the most accurate. That should be unthinkable for an intelligent woman.

DBN: It would be in any other situation.

TM: It would be in any other situation. One of the major points of *Paradise* is how to rate this community where everything—past, present, future—is locked to its citizens being pure black against this other community in which the members have nothing in common except gender, and you don't know who is white or black or mixed or not mixed. No reviewer has even mentioned this exercise.

DBN: It seems that in this book you have gotten away with saying all sorts of very direct truths. Somehow I don't think people will be happy with that. You don't soften things much.

TM: Well, this book was going to be called *War.*

DBN: From *War* to *Paradise*!

TM: Yes. Because it was about enormous conflicts that resolve themselves in assault, physical assault. That's what war is. The reasons people hurt each other. However, it was probably an unwise title, as my publishers persuaded me.

DBN: Why do you think they persuaded you not to use *War* as a title?

TM: Because it's not friendly? People would feel it was a bit harsh.

DBN: But what about *Beloved*? *Beloved* was very harsh.

TM: With *Beloved* I shifted the reader's attention to the ghost story and just gave the reader little tastes of slavery along the way. Because you couldn't take the brutality. It was overwhelming, like pornography or something. So I gave them a thing to play with: the relationship of Beloved to Sethe. Once Beloved entered the book, and it was clear that that was a fantastic thing, it distracted readers from this other thing, which was that this woman, Sethe, did not own her children. If you take Beloved out and just have Sethe running around with her daughter, its stark in ways you can't take.

DBN: The shameful thing for me is that I was taught to see slaves as anonymous, even though I'm black myself. How did you get such a clear sense of these individual people and their individual stories?

TM: I just investigated it. I learned a lot. Novel writing for me is an opportunity to learn about an issue I don't know a great deal about. I thought I knew a great deal about slavery until I started writing *Beloved*. Then you say: What?!" They did what?" It's overwhelming. And then you understand why your parents, your grandparents and everybody didn't talk about it. They didn't want you to know, because they don't think you can take it. They know that it's untake-able, and that you shouldn't be able to take it. They want your life geared to the future. So that whole business of remembering is an act of the will because you have to remember in order to forget.

DBN: It's truly traumatizing.

TM: Writing *Beloved* was very hard for me. Emotionally it was devastating. I would get up from the table and just walk until I could calm down enough to write the simple sentence.

DBN: What's the hardest sentence you had to write?

TM: "...little nigger-girl eyes staring between the wet fingers that held her face so her head wouldn't fall off." If they could live it, I can write it.

DBN: And we can read it. I studied *Beloved* in school and I found that a lot of the women, who were white, were down on Sethe. They couldn't see how she could kill her child. They felt she did not have the right. But I was thinking I could kill my child to spare her from slavery.

TM: Different black people responded to slavery differently. Some people were brave. Some people were not brave. Some of them ran away. Some people adopted the manners of the slave owner.

DBN: I like what you say about freedom in *Paradise*. "Here freedom was a test administered by the natural world that a man had to take for himself everyday and if he passed enough tests long enough he was king." I know you don't like to talk about your personal life, especially your divorce. But I did read where you said that even though divorce was painful you felt a certain kind of freedom. Could you talk about that?

TM: Freedom is when you are in a position to choose your responsibilities and every day you meet them. I don't want to be owned by somebody else. I don't want to be told what to do. Constantly. But in the case of being alone with children, there was a certain kind of liberation. It was very, very, very hard. Very hard. But it was like what Sethe said: it was me doing it. I call the shots. I'm that big. I can get all my children in my heart. And (when I became a single parent) it was something about me doing it, knowing at any moment I might fail, that I would have to go home and stay with my parents. They were fearful for me. But I had to try. I wasn't...jubilant. But I really felt...coherent...when I had to separate out my activities into those that helped my writing and my children, and those that did not.

DBN: In *Paradise* you write about a kind of macho masculine culture, but you often draw very tender male characters. You seem to like black men.

TM: One day a black man who taught at a university where I was reading said, "I tell all my students that you love black men." And I said, "Yes I do." But I get very annoyed because there are some people who accuse me of being anti-male. They act like I'm a sort of feminist kamikaze. And this becomes part of the public discourse. People ask me in Q & A sessions: "Why was Paul D. in *Beloved* such a wimp?" A wimp? Look at what that man survived. Intact. I really think men like to see themselves in wrestling terms. Like, Grrrr. The complexity of a man, particularly a black man, to me is just amazing. How they learn to be who they are...and the enormous obstacles to just being men, let alone being black men.

DBN: And yet they are the most beautiful creatures on the earth.

TM: They are the most beautiful creatures on the planet. And everyone loves them.

DBN: And everyone loves them.

TM: And are worried about them to the point of envy so great, so over-whelming, so large, that only in little ways do you see it dribble out, provided a black man doesn't say anything political. But even when he does say something political, there is still this adoration. They are the adored people of the earth.

DBN: I feel your novels come closest to offering me some sort of literary definition or theory of what constitutes black experience.

TM: I feel I haven't been able to articulate it in a satisfactory manner. I've sometimes thought there's a kind of an...exchange in the churches, in jazz and in music that black people do with each other. They antici-pate that the audience has some power in the performance. Therefore, when I write, I expect the audience to argue...to fuss...to defend...to do whatever in the book. It's not about just delivering something. It is about an interactive response. And I think that is part of the cultural phenomenon of the close association between an artist and the com-munity, the artist and the viewer, the artist and reader. A reviewer once said that I've been more influenced by James Joyce, and other modernist writers than by black culture. I don't know. My perceptions can be wrong. But the fact that I have them is the fact that I have them. I'm not sure enough about my ideas, however, to articulate them as a formula or even a theory of black art. The only thing I can do, is do it, and make certain kinds of assumptions about the work, about the people, about the race. One, of the first things I decided was that I didn't have to explain anything to a white reader. So that if I'm talking to you as a black person I could tell you all sorts of things that would depend heavily on your knowingness...not the historical knowingness...but just the interchange of language what this would mean, what that would mean. Culture. The other thing I decided was not to focus on the one-on-one white/ black confrontation issue, which has been the major focus of a lot of African-American fiction. One major exception to this has been Jean Toomer.

The point is I feel I can't fool black people. Now there are people who want me to fool them. They want me to write books in which all the black men are powerful and steady and moral and they never have a moment's doubt. But I am certain they want me to do that because they want white people to read it and think of them that way. There again the white gaze has penetrated.

Now it didn't with jazz and it didn't with a lot of art forms that were ours because we had to prove our value to each other. Those musicians were playing for each other and the mediocre ones just fell away. If I could use that analogy for writing: if I wrote so that a fastidious black reader would know everything, that would elevate the goal and elevate the writing.

DBN: With your novel *Jazz*, I think that was the first time I thought to myself these words are really reflecting black experience the way black music does, like notes, almost.

TM: *Jazz* was a very experimental book. I thought it was radical. Some people acknowledged certain things, like the whole ensemble feel and the notion that the narrator can not be relied upon to know the truth. No one person in a jazz combo is the only one. The most magnificent thing about watching Miles Davis is the long moments when he listens. To see him on stage listening to other musicians. Totally concentrating. And you know that whatever he heard he is going to have something to say about it when he next picks up that horn. It's the most democratic thing. It's amazing. In *Jazz* the narrator has to listen to the characters in order to tell the story. What the characters say may change what the narrator thinks they know.

DBN: I read that when you were a little girl you wanted to be a dancer like Maria Tallchief. Did you use to dance a lot? Did you study ballet?

TM: No I didn't study dance. We danced for other people. Me and my sister, and then me alone. She stopped because she got shy. I was six or five. I danced. At a party or a gathering like the Fourth of July we would all be dancing. If they saw one child that was good at these things they would display that child. I was good at dancing and I was good at storytelling. The adults would ask us to tell stories that they had told us many times. And we would repeat them and they would laugh like they were hearing them for the first time. It was a very performative thing. We didn't have television. For many years we didn't have radio. We had to sing, play the piano. My mother was a brilliant singer. My mother was a fabulous singer. She had the most beautiful human voice that I have ever heard. She was a soprano. And it made me not enjoy other singers. You know, I liked them but they were nothing like my mother. When I woke up I might hear her singing blues or she might be singing spirituals. She sang Carmen. She sang in church. She sang at every funeral. We were AME. But in my day people sang in the streets.

DBN: Music is everywhere in every book.

TM: I live up in Rockwood County and about three years ago I heard a male voice singing in the streets. And I ran upstairs and looked out the window and there was this black man coming down the street. He was delivering mail. I was smiling. He did that another mail delivery day, and then he stopped because the people complained. And that made me realize that I had been missing that for twenty, thirty years. That people sang. The iceman sang. The man with the horses and the drays sang, and the children.

DBN: That world you write about and sound nostalgic for—the black towns, the black clubs, the church, the community—that was really out there, right?

TM: Yes. That was real.

DBN: Is it gone?

TM: I think so.

DBN: Are you trying to bring it back?

TM: Some of it. The responsibility we felt for each other. All those mothers on the street, everybody who could tell you what to do as a child, who protected you. I remember I resented that type of intrusion then. But I miss it now.

Cecil Foster:
A Long Sojourn

Born in Barbados in 1954, Cecil Foster came to Canada in the late 1970s. His two novels deal with the social and psychological repercussions of immigration. In the highly acclaimed *No Man in the House* (1991) emigration promises young Howard Prescod escape from the deprivation of his Barbadian existence. *Sleep On, Beloved*, (1995) focuses on Ona Nedd, a Jamaican immigrant attempting to build a new life in Canada. His most recent book, *A Place Called Heaven: The Meaning of Being Black in Canada*, was published in 1996.

Donna Bailey Nurse: Describe growing up in Barbados. Was your life anything like Howard Prescod's?

Cecil Foster: Yes, on a superficial level. I grew up in a very poor neighbourhood, Lodge Road, where I set the book. There was me and two brothers and as in *No Man in the House*, my parents had gone off to England to live. I was the last of the three, somewhat like Howard. By the time you get into the third chapter or so, the resemblance to me has to some degree disappeared. I lived with my paternal grandmother from the time I was about 2 years old. Then I went to live with my maternal grandmother when I was about 11. Coming from both of them was the strong sense of extended family. Just about everybody was family: great-aunts, aunts, people who weren't blood relatives were, in effect, family—the extended family in the Caribbean. I also got a strong sense of the importance of education, it was seen as a way out. When I was growing up the ambitious ones among us saw ourselves as emigrants in the making. I can still remember the headmaster at my school teaching us about past students who had done well abroad. Very often it was used as a negative form of socializing for us, too. If you ran into problems with the law, that could finish your chances of getting overseas.

DBN: You started working as a reporter when you were still in Barbados. Did you always hope to enter that field?

CF: I always wanted to be a writer. I don't remember much of my youth. I don't know if I'm repressing it or what, because I had a tough time. But there are some parts that I remember, like going to school to write an essay and my bigger brother seeing it and pulling my leg. I was talking then about becoming a communicator. I remember another occasion, too. In Barbados at the end of every school year you didn't automatically get promoted; you had to sit an exam. It was a very bright afternoon. I was in the darkened hall, looking out into the glaring bright afternoon sun, beyond the escarpment and onto the blue Atlantic Ocean. One essay topic was "What would you like to be when you grow up?" And I remember sitting there and writing that I wanted to be a writer. I would have been about 13.

DBN: I read that you weren't really into reading until you were about 12 years old.

CF: It became mandatory to go to the library. We would go in on the appointed day, look for a book, take it home and toss it aside, and then take it back without ever reading it. I remember going to the library and doing the thing that everyone else did: look for the slimmest book I could find. I intended to go home and throw it aside and play cricket. Something must have happened, though, and my grandmother kept me in the house. And she said "Well, you went to the library. Why don't you read your book?" So I picked up this book, *Amongst Thistles and Thorns* by Austin Clarke, and by the light of the lamp I started to read it. I was sitting in the corner and other people were out in the backyard talking. And I thought Gee! This is about a boy just like me. One of the characters, the little boy, ran away from home in rebellion against his mother. And at that point, I guess, I really felt like rebelling too, because my grandmother had kept me in the house and I was angry. I identified with the book right off the top. And that was my introduction to West Indian literature. From then on that was all I would read. I really fell in love with the writers from Trinidad, Mark Anthony and others like V.S. Naipaul.

DBN: You describe Austin Clarke as your mentor. What is it that you admire so much about him?

CF: What I admire is the fact that he stuck it out in this city and now has published about fifteen books. Austin has not got the attention that is his due. There are white writers who have written less than Austin and who have not been writing as perceptively about the Canadian experience, and they win the accolades. Many people would have gone to the States. And to think that, for a while, he was the only published black author around. I mean, who did he feed on, who did he discuss things with? I would think that for him it was usually a case of people coming to say, "Austin-boy, how can I get this manuscript published?" as opposed to sitting down with people he might have rightfully called his peers. I think that Austin may have suffered because there wasn't the kind of intellectual discourse going on that would allow people to put his work in another context or put it up against somebody else's work. It was standing alone all the time. I enjoy going into Austin's house and having one of his famous martinis and sitting down and talking, because as a young writer I can learn. And I often say to him, "Well, Austin, it used to be you alone. Who did you talk to?" And he would say,"Yes, yes." But he doesn't really talk much about it. I think that ultimately his earlier works are going to be rediscovered. That trilogy: *The Meeting Point*, *Storm of Fortune* and *The Bigger Light* , constitutes a seminal work of the immigrant experience.

DBN: *No Man in the House* is a coming-of-age story quite similar to Austin Clarke's *Amongst Thistles and Thorns*. Would you say this novel influenced yours?

CF: In Barbados there are three books that deal with that type of story: You have *In the Castle of My Skin* by George Lamming, which dealt with a coming-of-age situation in the 1930s. And then you have Austin's *Amongst Thistles and Thorns*, which dealt with the same subject in the 1950s, and *No Man in the House* which dealt with it in the 1960s. If you read the three of them together you would have a pretty good idea of how life has gone in the Caribbean generationally over thirty or forty years. So I'm looking forward to reading the work of people who can say, "This is my experience as a person of Barbadian Independence."

DBN: In Barbados you had a promising career as a journalist. Why did you decide to leave?

CF: I felt that emigration was in my plans one way or the other. Then I ran into some problems at home because of my writing. I guess I was an overly ambitious journalist in Barbados. I wrote a report from the House of Assembly that the government didn't like, so they made life a little uncomfortable for me at the time. I came up here in '79 with $750. I saw that money quickly running out, so I started to sell encyclopedias. I don't think there were any weeks I took home more than the minimum wage because I was absolutely terrible at it. After that I got a couple of lucky breaks. I decided to offer my services to *Contrast* (a black community newspaper in Toronto from the '60s to the '80s). At that time the editor had just left. I went to talk to a man there named Al Hamilton, who offered me the job. This was during a fascinating period when there was one very infamous police shooting (Albert Johnson), and the black community was really up in arms. I got to meet and talk to the people and feel the anger. *Contrast* was also a sort of community centre. People dropped in and we had meetings. At that time, the National Black Coalition of Canada had its office upstairs from *Contrast*. It was sort of an NAACP Association, led by people like Howard McCurdy and Al Mercury.

So we had all of this energy going, and a lot of young immigrants waiting to take on the world. Some of the leading black journalists of today were there: Royson James, who is at the *Star*, and Hamelin Grange, of the CBC. *Contrast* also taught me something that I remember quite vividly. When I first came here, Oakland Ross was writing a feature on the black community. He came to me and said, "There's a lot of debate going on as to whether blacks want to be called African, Caribbean, black or what." So—call it a bit of nationalism—I opened my mouth and out jumped the words, "As far as I see myself, I see myself as a Bajan first, a West Indian second, and a black man third." At that time I was a recent immigrant, so I didn't see myself as Canadian. I felt quite good, I had been quoted in the *Globe*. I went to *Contrast* and as soon as I walked through the door everyone said, "Are you crazy? How can you say something like that?" They said, "This island thing, this American thing, has to go. This is one of the biggest holdbacks to black people in this country. Ultimately, what we have in common is that we are all African and black." I believe I was wrong—very wrong. And I am very grateful that they dumped on me.

DBN: Is there a black Canadian literary aesthetic emerging and if so how would you describe it?

CF: I would say there is a black aesthetic. When I go to poetry readings, I see it in the anger and the fire and in the sense of saying, "We belong here. We are going to fight back and we are not going to run away. We are going to make sure that there is change." I see it, too, in how they present themselves; how words, music, rhythm all interplay to create a cultural thing, an artistic thing. We have a phenomenal outpouring of work from black writers. Look at people like Austin Clarke, Dionne Brand, Afua Cooper, Ayanna Black. Think of the people published in those anthologies Ayanna Black has brought out in the last two years [*Fiery Spirits and Voices*]; there is a vibrant black writing community in Toronto. There are also writers in Montreal and Edmonton and Ottawa and other places. Getting access to mainstream publishing is obviously still a big problem. Sometimes I feel that what is happening in the black community is reminiscent of what was happening in England in the

1950s and '60s, when West Indian literature came into vogue. And we are now beginning to feel settled and beginning to look back upon the region we came from and write about the environment in which we now find ourselves.

DBN: In a recent issue of *This Magazine* Andre Alexis suggests that black Canadian artists have developed African-American sensibilities in place of a strong Canadian consciousness. Would you agree?

CF: It's an interesting discussion. But I think that it is the kind of discussion where you can end up blaming the victim. The fact that we don't have an overwhelming body of black literature isn't because there haven't been writers over the ages. George Elliott Clarke has proven with his anthology *Fire on the Water* that from way back that body of literature was out there, but it never got published and never got sustained. Also I do not have any problem whatsoever in laying claim to black icons from any place in the world. I feel they are all common property and we can use them. Should I disown a Nelson Mandela? Should I disown a Martin Luther King or a Malcolm X? Other cultures don't. English writers—even those who are living in Canada—can deal with Chaucer and Shakespeare.

DBN: What about the argument that African-American culture fails to reflect accurately the Black Canadian experience?

CF: The reality for many blacks in Canada may be closer to what they see in the streets of New York or Los Angeles than what many people assume as being their reality. Black youth here are offered images of Wayne Gretzky and others as heroes. I'm sure many of them would prefer to have a Michael Jordan over a Wayne Gretzky. Why? Because there is the feeling that here is a black man who has triumphed. They do not identify with a Wayne Gretzky. How can they?

DBN: You often speak about writers as prophets and recorders. Is that how you see your task?

CF: Perhaps the writer's task is to keep challenging the community, to record and also to prophesy. James Baldwin saw himself as a writer who, at times, if you can use the analogy of the prophet, not only foretold but also had the unenviable task of speaking directly to his people and saying: "You'd better get your house in order." Very often it wasn't an easy message to deliver. And sometimes it was a message that was brought at great peril and personal loss to the prophet.

DBN: What did you want to communicate to your readers in *Sleep On, Beloved*?

CF: What I'm arguing in that book is that multiculturalism can work. That multiculturalism worked in the Caribbean where we had people from different places getting along and that the best form of multiculturalism is when you allow people to be natural. So Grandma Nedd (a Pocomanian) was always natural. She danced the way she wanted to dance. She did not debauch herself. She danced for her God. And whereas the pastor would always hope to convert the Rastafarians into Pocomanians, she never did. She was very accepting of them. I also wanted to talk about how we move away from the spirituality that was ours. First of all, we had Grandma Nedd dancing for her God, and then we had Ona dancing for secular reasons, and ultimately we had Suzanne table dancing for money. It's also an indication of what has happened to us as immigrants. The reason most of us left the Caribbean was economic, to get a better job or a better life for our children. In essence we became whores, no different from, say Suzanne dancing for money. As economic refugees, to some degree, we start to go for the dollar at all costs. In the book, one of the big problems was that Ona felt that being a West Indian was baggage that held her back. She wanted to sublimate who the heck she was. My argument is that we don't need to change that drastically, because even when we do, we don't get the dream.

DBN: What is the dream?

CF: One of the dreams in Caribbean fiction is "Where is home for the nigger?" Because, certainly in the previous generation, there wasn't an acceptance of the Caribbean as home. So where is home, really? Is home back in Africa? Is home in a new Caribbean that we are supposedly developing at a time of Independence? Or is it a place like Canada which can be a multicultural society? I guess to some degree I'm toying with the idea and arguing that a multicultural Canada could be home; or it could be a place where we could make a long sojourn. [*Books in Canada*, 1995]

Lawrence Hill:
In Black and White

Lawrence Hill is the author of the novels *Any Known Blood* (1997) and *Some Great Thing* (1992). His latest book, *Black Berry Sweet Juice: On Being Black and White in Canada* (2001), bravely examines the experiences of interracial families. One of Hill's main projects is the excavation of black Canadian history. Two of his books in particular reflect this concern: *Trials and Triumphs: The Story of African Canadians* (1993) and *Women of Vision: The Story of the Canadian Negro Women's Association* (1996). I first met Larry in the early 1980s when we both worked as interviewers for the Ontario Black History Society. He is a sharp, passionate, socially conscious man and a devoted father of three. He belongs to an accomplished family. His late father, Daniel Hill, Sr. was a prominent social activist and a former Ombudsman of the city of Toronto. His older brother Dan, is a renowned singer/songwriter. Larry visited me at my apartment near the waterfront in Toronto.

Donna Bailey Nurse: Tell me about your parents.

Lawrence Hill: Well my parents are both American-born. My father was born in Independence, Missouri in 1923. My mother was born in South Dakota but raised in Oak Park, Illinois, Hemingway country. She was born in 1928. My mother is white, my father's black. My mother and father are from fairly religious backgrounds. My father was raised by an African Methodist Episcopal minister and moved around all over the States through his childhood because his father changed cities every couple of years. He was only in Missouri for the first six months of his life. Then he moved to Kansas. Then they were out in Denver and California. In his school years my father was primarily in the Western States and there wasn't a sufficiently large black population in places like Denver, Portland and Berkeley to justify segregated schools. So his schooling was integrated just because he was in communities that had only small amounts of black people. As a result, when he did hit the US Army in the Second World War, which was a grossly segregated experience, he grew to really hate it.

Of course, it was the old thing that you are good enough to die for your country, but not to live in an integrated society. After the army he went off for a year to study at the University of Oslo in Norway and that was a huge turning point for him, because he saw a world where he felt accepted and where race wasn't thrown in his face every moment of every day. And he had social mobility. It opened his eyes up to other possibilities. When he came back from that year abroad I think his mind was made up that one way or another he was going to leave the United States. It was not a country he was going to stay in.

I don't think that we can minimize the gravity of these positions. I mean to leave your country—especially to leave the United States—it's not as if you're fleeing for economic reasons. You're fleeing on a matter of racial principle which is a whole different sort of psychological mindset.

My Dad came to U of T and did some graduate work. He went back to teach for a year in Baltimore before returning to U of T to do his doctorate. He met my mother the year he was teaching in Baltimore. She had a job with a democratic senator in the US congress and she was sort of a civil rights activist. They met and fell in love and married and came to Toronto in 1953.

DBN: It's interesting that despite his antipathy towards America, your father did marry an American.

LH: But he married an American who was totally engaged in his struggle. She was probably in some ways more militant than he was. He wasn't living as an activist, she was. He was obviously the source of more racial discrimination being black. But she was the one who was committed to a lifestyle of protest and that showed itself in every aspect of her living.

DBN: Didn't your mother once say that she could never have married anyone who was not Jewish or black?

LH: Basically it would have been hard for her to imagine marrying somebody who wasn't Jewish or black or in some way a member of a minority group who had to fight. She had trouble imagining a traditional white man as a partner.

So they very much fell in love. She was from a Protestant, very Republican background. Her parents and grandparents on both sides were quite Conservative farmer types. Her father was a writer and a pharmacist. A writer on pharmaceutical issues. But very conservative.

DBN: So how did she develop such open-minded attitudes?

LH: She felt that one of the turning points had to do with her church affiliation. The pastor at her church was very much in favour of integration. There was a big fight in the church because a black family wanted to join. The pastor said he'd leave if they weren't let in. He won this fight. I think my mother was very influenced by other people around her who were in her eyes progressive and who met the longings of her own soul.

My mother really grew up in the generation—and she still talks about this—where she thought: "What can I do for the world? How can I serve my country?" And she still talks in a lamenting way about how people just don't talk like that anymore.

She studied sociology at a university that very much upheld the principles of equality of opportunity, Oberlin College. So my parents were clearly well-matched in terms of their world view.

DBN: How do you feel your parents impacted on the person you became?

LH: I felt I had a view of different worlds from the same family vantage point. I marvelled that I might be in a black environment among black family friends and relatives in the morning and then move into some utterly white environment in the afternoon. These transitions always struck me as being stark. But I felt privileged, I suppose, to be able to move in what I felt were different worlds socially. I guess I felt that I was raised by people who taught me to try to look critically at the world around me, to think critically about things I read or was told and to use my judgment and to trust it.

DBN: You seemed to have a pretty clear idea of your identity when you were growing up.

LH: I felt pretty clear. There were a few moments when I went through turmoil which we all do and I can talk about those. At the point where I really started to think about racial identity issues, around 12 to 14, I felt clearly what I was interested in and what I wanted to do. I hadn't necessarily found my place yet, but I knew what I was passionate about. I had no ambiguity about how interested I was in reading black literature as a way of learning more about the black experience and embracing it in some way. It was one of the few ways available to me because I wasn't in a physical black community.

DBN: What books did you read?

LH: I read everything in my parent's bookshelves. *Invisible Man* [by Ralph Ellison]. James Baldwin novels. Richard Wright's books, like *The*

Black Boy. There weren't many prominent black women writers yet. Remember this was the late 1970s. But that stuff I started getting to as it came out. I certainly read everything they had of Langston Hughes. I think they had some poetry of Countee Cullen.

DBN: What did you read of Langston Hughes?

LH: I remember his novel *Not Without Laughter* which is openly autobiographical and about living in Kansas as a boy.

DBN: There are so many allusions to Langston Hughes in your novel *Any Known Blood*. Your writing shares with his a particular buoyancy.

LH: Yes there's a buoyancy and also a certain unapologetic ambiguity in some of Langston Hughes' poetry, ambiguity about racial identity and anger, mixed in with humour. And certainly his approach to anger and bitterness, some outrageously funny sections, appealed to me a great deal.

I've always looked for a way to write about things that were serious to me in an entertaining manner. My father was a tremendous storyteller. An amazing storyteller. He had great timing. He knew how to withhold a detail until you were just salivating for it, and even in the pacing and the intonation, he knew how to draw us in. His stories were ribald and raucous and fairly impossible. And they were often man against beast kind of stories. Or they were stories that entertained us because of their complete implausibility. But they were very gripping. He told a lot of stories about his work environments as well. He would come home after work and tell us about crazy people he had met or really interesting situations or he'd recreate some real dilemma at work that he'd been in and ask: "Well what would you do Larry? Or what do you think I did? Or how would you have handled this? He was quite entertaining in that aspect of his parenting and he stimulated our love of story and our love of drama, even though he didn't realize what he was doing.

I also read all the stuff by Eldridge Cleaver [*Soul on Ice*] and of course that was disturbing. He wrote in a very passionate, powerful manner and he speculated openly about some of the negative motivations that would bring a black man and a white woman together. He forced me to think about these things when I perhaps wasn't entirely ready to do so. He did some very ugly things and thought in some very ugly ways, but he wrote with such power that I had to grapple with that: "He's writing so powerfully, but is it right? Does it make sense? Do I buy into this? What does this mean about my parents?" A little later *Roots* [by Alex Haley] came along. Also *The Autobiography of Malcolm X*. And so those were some of the books that made up my early reading.

DBN: You have a very solid style. Your books could almost run on structure alone. Where did you study your craft?

LH: Actually, my literary education in a formal sense is kind of pitiful. I had some terrific high school English teachers who I loved and who loved me. One of them in particular encouraged me to write a lot. And I was writing short stories by the time I was 14 or so. These stories weren't required for school. I would write them on my mother's Elsie Smith typewriter which was so big it could have been a weapon in war if you dropped it on somebody from a height. I would bash away at it. She had it in the family room. And that's where I worked. And she used it and I used it and my brother Dan used it. And we had typing contests to see who could type the fastest, my brother and I. I learned to type on a typewriter that had the keyboard blackened out in grade eight. The teacher would bash our fingers with a ruler if we looked at the keys. But also there were no letters on the keys so there was no point looking down. I knew in grade eight that I absolutely had to learn to type really well. So I became a very proficient typist quite early. I wrote and wrote and wrote on that sucker. My mother was one of the first readers of my stuff and she was always highly critical. She never really jumped up and down with praise, but usually would point out all the mistakes. I may have showed it to one or two friends here and there but it was primarily my mother who would read this stuff.

DBN: You knew you wanted to be a writer?

LH: Well, I knew I wanted to write. I didn't walk around saying to myself when I was 14 that I wanted to be a writer, I just knew I wanted to write. That's how I thought of it.

DBN: What kind of stories did you write?

LH: Stories about racial identity. I think my first story was about a black boy falling in love with a white girl and running off to North Carolina. Romantic stories of racial peril. They were pretty awful. They weren't going anywhere. I wasn't writing for school. I was just writing them.

I had a track coach who became a very close friend of mine and a personal mentor. He really became a father figure. I probably spent much more time with him in my teenage years than my father. I was a competitive runner. Not very good but very serious. This track coach was a reporter at the *Toronto Star*, Dave Steen. Because he was a writer at the *Star*, I used to show him my stories, and he used to just tear them apart from a standpoint of style and editing. He took me into the *Toronto Star* and showed me around and I was blown away by the newsroom. How people could sit in such chaos and write. It was just typewriters then. I was quite impressed by that and I gave him my stuff and he would always hack it apart mercilessly just the way an editor at a newspaper would. I think it was a bit of overkill actually. I wouldn't quite take that approach if I were encouraging a 13 or 14 year old to write. But it made me a better writer. It made me a better stylist.

DBN: Did it help you learn to take criticism?

LH: Absolutely. I learned early. Here was a man that I loved and I knew he loved me totally. But he ripped my stuff to shreds. That toughened me up. I studied a bit of creative writing at university. I had a terrific teacher in second year, Douglas Banks. He was a writer himself. And that really got me fired up. Much as I enjoyed the creative writing courses, and sharing myself in a workshop situation, I wanted to study something else. I wanted to broaden my world. So I ended up doing a degree in Economics which I found quite interesting. It served me well. Later on, I worked for several years as a newspaper reporter for the *Globe* and for the *Winnipeg Free Press* and I often wrote about economic issues.

I started at UBC in Vancouver and finished off the degree two years later in Quebec city at Laval University. That's where I graduated. I wanted to become totally, fluently, bilingual. That was very important to me, so I made that happen by going to live and study in French.

DBN: Why was becoming bilingual so important to you?

LH: I was absolutely passionate about that from my early years. I knew I wanted to become completely bilingual. My mother was excited about the idea. She'd loved studying French when she was at university in the States and often spoke to us in little sentences here and there. Her French wasn't very good but she was excited about it. My sister and I both became completely fluent. Also my best friend's mother was French Canadian and their family was completely bilingual. So my childhood best friend was a guy who moved back and forth fluidly in English and French the way that Trudeau would.

So university didn't have very much to do with my literary development. Much later, about ten years ago or so, I went back to do an M.A. in creative writing at Johns Hopkins in Baltimore, but by then I was a writer. I had published a novel, *Some Great Thing*, that came out in 1992, the same year I was studying at Johns Hopkins. I started there in September and the book was published in September. There were some terrific teachers there. John Barth was one of them. One of his books is downstairs in your lobby here and I was chuckling as I was looking through it because it is totally clever with wordplay. Not highly accessible, but funny in an intellectual kind of way.

The teacher that really blew me away at John Hopkins was Stephen Dixon. He's not that well known, although he's published hundreds of short stories and has been nominated for the National Book award. Apart from being a very prodigious—he publishes about a book a year—Dixon is also an amazing teacher. He influenced me a lot as a teacher. Just the way he rolls his sleeves up in a totally disarming and unpretentious way and gets right in there with your work.

DBN: Do you teach?

LH: Occasionally. I don't teach at the university now, but I frequently work with students and I am right now working with high school students through this writers in electronic residence program. I've done that for years, on and off. Occasionally I teach for a week at a university. Occasionally, I take on one or two people as mentors and work with them to help them along. I've taught at Johns Hopkins for a year and at Ryerson for a year. I've taught a lot. And, if I do say so myself, I'm a very good teacher. I like to work with people who are trying to write and I have a lot to share with them.

DBN: Can it be taught, then, in your opinion?

LH: You can't teach creative genius, but there is a great deal that can be taught. Would you expect a painter to develop in complete isolation from other painters? The word "teaching" is a little misleading. It's not like sitting up in a physics class and teaching theories and formulae and so forth. But there is a great deal that can be taught.

DBN: Do you socialize a lot with other writers?

LH: I have a few friends who are writers. But as a single dad, working for a living, I don't have a whole lot of spare time. I'm not a socialite kind of guy. For a few years before I was published I met with Oakland Ross and a few others for a few years and we shared each other's stuff every few weeks. But it wasn't a bar hopping or social thing. We'd sit down and show each other our stuff and read each other's work and help each other along.

I've met a lot of writers because I've contributed here and there and gotten involved with the Writers Union of Canada and the National Council a couple of years ago. And obviously through writerly functions

I've met a lot of writers over the years. Most of us tend to know each other pretty quickly. Canada is a fairly small country. So through book tours and through readings and through volunteer work with the Writers Union and PEN I've met a lot of writers. But I don't hang out with them. And only a few writers are good friends of mine and that's mostly to do with childhood relationships.

DBN: Like who?

LH: Paul Quarrington is a close friend and we've been friends since childhood. We were friends before either of us knew we were going to be writers.

DBN: Are you making a good living from your novels?

LH: The most I've ever had from a book is maybe a year of grace time, which isn't too bad considering a year is a fair amount of expenses with three kids. Apart from that I've had to cram it in on the side.

DBN: Are you working on a novel right now?

LH: Yes.

DBN: Would you like to talk about it?

LH: Not on the record.

DBN: I thought *Black Berry, Sweet Juice* was a really brave book. Race is such a difficult subject. Was it difficult to produce the book with a white editor?

LH: Well, I like my editor. Her name is Iris Tupholme, with HarperCollins. She's got a great personality. And one of the things I like about Iris, is I think she knows how to talk to me to encourage me or inspire me to go back to the drawing board and do my own stuff. Iris is not a hands-on get all up in your face editor. She encourages you to maybe go back to the drawing board to write with more depth about this, or to fill that out. She's not very directive. Maybe she is with others, but she's not with me. She does have a very good instinct about how to get me going. She knows how to do that in a way that doesn't interfere with my desires, and actually excites them.

Really though, Iris is the editor and I am the writer and the book is produced by me and I take complete responsibility for it. And it's not as if I have an editor telling me what to do, or integrally involved from the conception of the book. I mean I put together a book and say here it is and then we work to improve it and then bring it through the last yards to get it ready and that's a very important process and it makes the final product much better. But basically it's my book and it comes out of my heart and my soul and my mind and intellect and my fingers. I think for me I wouldn't express it in terms of "How would I work with a white editor?" Basically I'm working with myself and I happen to have a white editor close to the end of the process.

DBN: I don't think I mean it the way you think I mean it. I think editing is a conversation, just like the one you're talking about. And I think race is a hard conversation to have.

LH: It is. It is a hard conversation. And the response to black writers reiterates how difficult that conversation can be. *Black Berry* was a tough book to go public with. I thought it was maybe mildly scary to write the thing. But if I'd known how tough it would be to go public with it I would have been more scared, and it's a good thing I didn't really anticipate that. It was my third book to have any significant public interest. *Some Great Thing*, *Any Known Blood* and *Black Berry, Sweet Juice*. It was the first time that I toured and I didn't so much enjoy the process. It was a difficult process. It's one thing to stand up and talk about novels, to read from a novel. You always have a protective veil separating you from the novel. People aren't supposed to make easy autobiographical assumptions based on what's in the novel. Some people may. And you consider that they are a little bit gauche and you can set them straight. But here I was pouring out very intimate stuff and very intimate family stuff, some of it upsetting to my family, which you sort of have to do if you are writing honestly about family issues. Who's going to be pleased by that? I certainly wouldn't be happy if one of my children came to me in fifteen years and said they were writing a family story of some sort.

So it was hard to do family-wise. It was hard to do publicly. It was hard to talk about it. And it was hard to stand up and speak over and over again publicly about the most intimate of issues. Aside from a few close friends, I'm actually a quiet and cautious person. And I don't share a great deal of my private life with the world. But when I write, I do, of course. Because that's how I have to write. And so, here I was, outing myself in a way. And whether I was ready or not I had to do this. It was my own book and you have to promote your own book.

DBN: Well, what was so painful about it? What did people ask you that disturbed you?

LH: It wasn't what people ask me that disturbed me. It's just that I wasn't emotionally ready to stand up, every day for months, and talk about private issues of racial identity. It's the sort of thing that maybe you chew over once every six months with somebody...and then you put it aside and let it go for a while. You don't necessarily focus on these things on a day to day basis when you are just carrying out your life—as a writer, as a parent, working, commuting, moving kids around, exercising. All the things you might do in a day normally if you are a healthy person not normally preoccupied with your racial identity. It would drive you crazy. And who needs that? And to be focused on that every second of the day would be very unfortunate. But when you are on tour talking every day about it, it's exhausting. You don't always want to stand up at ten in the morning and talk about the identity struggles you had when you were 14 years old to somebody who doesn't have a clue about it and who may react antagonistically or may not. So it wasn't so much the questions—although there were a few doozies—it was just the stress of having to expose myself on intimate issues. That's what was tough.

DBN: I thought the book was brave because I didn't know whether or not Canadians were ready for that conversation.

LH: Well, I heard that over and over again. People said they cringed when they read certain things. And certain things are sort of taboo. But why should they be? Surely the job of a writer is to try to go for things, whether people want to hear them or not.

You know what? It does open up the world and people do start talking more about these things. Barriers have been broken. I think there is some talking going on as a result of *Black Berry* that maybe wouldn't have happened without it. So I feel it was a good thing to do. I by no means feel that it was a perfect book, or that it couldn't have been better. But I'm happy that I did it. It was a good step along the way. It's part of my literary tool kit and I'm glad it's there.

DBN: Your heritage is both black and white, both Canadian and American. How do you think this contributes to your way of perceiving the world? What a hard question...

LH: I don't know if I am the best person to answer that question.

DBN: You're the only person I know who can answer it.

LH: Look, I'm interested in the world and I come at it from a variety of perspectives. I'm interested in exploring issues of identity, among them racial identity. I am very interested in the relationship between Canada and the United States and the relationship between people in both countries historically and now. I think the war—if you want to call it that—or the assault on Iraq is a crime against humanity and at the same time I have American relatives in the US Army whom I love very much and who I would not want to see killed in battle. My allegiances are multitudinous and they cross all sorts of boundaries and nationalities and racial groups. I guess we all are complicated people and we all have different strands of our personalities, that are informed by different origins. In my case, perhaps those strands are a little more palpable or visible than in the cases of some other people. They have made me the curious and energetic and happily ambivalent person that I am about the world and about the issues that fascinate me. I can't think of a better career for me than to be a writer. But I'm also very engaged on a daily basis as a father and as a citizen and in other personal relationships and I think, really, the writer part of me is just one of many parts. And those aspects of my identity—Canadian/American and black/white—inform every part of my being, not just that writing part. [Toronto, 2003]

David Odhiambo:
African Perspectives

David Odhiambo was born in Nairobi, Kenya in 1965 and settled in Canada in the mid-1970s. He is the author of two novels, *diss/ed banded nation* (1998) and *Kipligat's Chance* (2003). Odhiambo's play *Afrocentric* (1996) has been produced in Vancouver, Calgary and Toronto. After graduating from McGill University, Odhiambo spent time working with street kids in Vancouver. This concern for the disenfranchised permeates his work. His blend of African perspectives, wry humour and social consciousness is wholly unique in Canadian fiction. I met Odhiambo for breakfast at the Westin Harbour Castle in Toronto on an icy morning in spring 2003.

Donna Bailey Nurse: Your novel *Kipligat's Chance* is set in Kenya. Is that where you were born and raised?

David Odhiambo: I was born in Kenya in 1965. I don't remember the first few years of my life. When I was 5 I went to boarding school about five hundred miles away from home. My father was an evangelist preacher, so I got a scholarship. For the first two years I was there I was so scared. When I look back on this time, one of the things I remember is that that was the first time I heard of the atom bomb. A bomb that could destroy the entire world. I remember being worried about that.

The school was just beginning to integrate. I was one of the few African students and I think that experience was eye-opening. The country had been independent for about seven years and that colonial mentality was still very much a part of life.

DBN: When you say the schools were just beginning to integrate, you mean black people were finally beginning to be included in the country's social life, just like here in North America?

DO: Yes, and it would have been the same in other African countries. At school, teachers would call you stupid, and other students would say the same thing, and that was a holdover from colonialism.

DBN: Did you believe them, when they called you stupid?

DO: I think that somewhere inside I've always been very independent and I think I had a sense of myself that was very different from everything that I was hearing. I didn't believe them. I was there for four years and then I went to another school closer to home. I lived at home. And then when I was 12, I went to boarding school in Winnipeg. I had a relative there. I often hear people complain about the experience of coming to Canada, but I was never able to relate to that experience, that sense of strangeness or culture shock. I just remember the sky being really, really blue.

DBN: Bluer than in Kenya?

DO: It was just that prairie sky.

DBN: Could you say a little more about your family?

DO: I'm from a large family. There are five of us. I am right in the middle. My parents worked for an evangelical organization. My father travelled a lot and preached a lot. My mother was in the office managing. They were Baptists and I just remember going to church twice a day on Sundays. The one thing I admired about my parents is that they had a palpable sense of God. For a while, actually, that's what I thought I would do. I'd be a preacher. When I was about 13—I'm a little bit embarrassed about the fact now—I used to witness.

DBN: Don't be embarrassed with me. I get it. Oprah used to witness. Do you still have that faith?

DO: Well, I think that it evolved to become something else. I went through this period when I was in university, when the world was becoming much larger to me. Suddenly, I had all these feelings and that became more interesting to me than my prayers and my readings of the Bible. And at a certain point I started to read Nietzsche. His arguments against the existence of God made a lot of sense to me. I think at that point I shifted. I don't know what I've become now. But I have a fundamental faith in the power of love.

DBN: What do you remember of your physical surroundings in Kenya?

DO: Well this is difficult to say because when I was there, there was so much political fighting, religious too. My father was constantly in danger.

DBN: Why?

DO: By the time I was about 5 or 6 they were wealthy. And I think that as a result they became targets.

DBN: Of who?

DO: It was one of those odd experiences where people don't drive at night, because they are scared of car jackings. For me there was just always a fear. Looking back that's one of the things I appreciate getting away from. But I really miss the beauty of the landscape. I went back to Kenya a year after I came to Winnipeg and I knew that it would most likely be the last time I was going to be in the country. I spent the entire time just trying to soak everything up. Actually the school that I ended up going to until the age of 12 was right next door to Nairobi National Park. On the way to school there would be giraffes and zebra. Sometimes lions would come onto the school grounds.

DBN: That's awesome. Did the experience give you a sense of your place in nature?

DO: I really think it's a sense of belonging to something larger. Yes I think that's it. Like in Nairobi at night, the stars in the sky are so bright and when there is a thunderstorm there is just a real sense that you're in danger. The thunder is so loud. And the lightning, it just seems like it marks the entire sky.

DBN: When we North American blacks think of Africa we think of the historical slave experience. But that slave experience does not belong to you who are African-born, which is in some ways ironic. Instead, it belongs to those blacks who were transported out of Africa. How does not having that slave experience in your history contribute to your work? Do you ever think about this?

DO: I do actually think about it. I grew up in a country where the majority of the people are black. So I think that black became a norm. It was a big change for me to come here and be in the minority. I think that absolutely means that I take something for granted. I don't think it's particularly important to me to figure out who I am. Because I think I quite early had derived some understanding that I am black.

The slave narrative is something I explored in my early twenties. But it's not something that I'd like to write about. George Elliott Clarke, who I admire, writes about slavery in Canada and I think Austin Clarke talks about slavery in *The Polished Hoe*. But I don't think the subject matter of slavery holds me.

DBN: Do you feel any guilt about that?

DO: I did, a couple of years ago. But now I know I just have to write what I'm compelled by. I'm fairly interested in contemporary, urban, black culture. So I write about that.

DBN: That's great because I often think black Canadian men write about what they think they should write about and not what is really on their minds.

DO: Well I got to a place where I was feeling anxious and I thought to myself, if I am anxious about this perhaps it will need to be explored. I realized that part of the reason I was feeling anxious was because I was writing flawed black characters, I wasn't creating role models.

DBN: There is that pressure on black writers. I read that two of your favourite authors are J.D. Salinger and Mordecai Richler.

DO: Yes, that's true. To write this book I did a lot of reading. I actually started with the early novels like *Robinson Crusoe* and I worked my way through Jane Austen and some Dickens. D.H. Lawrence was the point at which I started to get excited. Lawrence was doing something with dialect. The world in his novels was allowing different people to speak.

DBN: What did you get from reading Lawrence?

DO: I guess part of it was courage. I have a hard time with James Joyce. His short story "The Dead" is the short story I like most. What I like about his work is that he is ambitious. That's what I got from reading him. I read some Sartre. I read *Nausea*. It's actually a wonderfully constructed book. Sartre tried to do something with writing where he wrote in real time. He allowed the novel to be an exploration of how things unfold. By the time I got back to Salinger I had the background of all these other books. What I liked about *Catcher in the Rye* was the way Salinger allowed the character to exist in the present. There isn't much reference to the past. One thing I saw was that for a white audience there is an assumption of a shared history. That's intially what started me exploring with [the character] Leeds in *Kipligat's Chance*. I initially wanted to stay in the present. But I eventually realized there was a necessity to bring in the past.

DBN: I did notice in the book that there was an awareness of the past but that you did not want it to overwhelm the present.

DO: I did need the past, but just to help provide a context for the characters to be able to live in the present.

DBN: What made you decide that you wanted to read so much before plunging into *Kipligat's Chance*?

DO: I am really intrigued by the craft of writing and what I can learn from the past in order to bring something new to the future of writing. I'm also aware of some African-Canadian writers and I'm interested in seeing if I can push the work in a new direction. One of the things that I hesitated to do was write with humour. But after I read Mordecai Richler *Barney's Version*, I thought, I'm going to go for it.

DBN: Like that hilarious scene when Svetlana's father goes after Leeds with a bat because he doesn't want her dating a black man.

DO: Yes. I think it's very difficult to write about painful things but still allow a person to laugh at the absurdity.

DBN: Who do you think is going to be offended by your humour?

DO: Well, when I started writing in the early 1990s there was a real constriction around what people could say. A man writing female characters was a problem. Taking points of view that might be considered less than radical, I think was looked down upon. I went through that and was hindered by it. But as I've gotten older my confidence level has improved. I've decided that I'm young right now and perhaps I can just write unabashedly. When I look back I can just chalk it up to my youth.

DBN: Good plan. You do use humour and ridicule often to get your point across. Like in *Kipligat's Chance*, when Leeds' boss at the furniture store tells him he is setting a bad example for his race. That was another very funny scene.

DO: I think our identity as a community is very much connected to our anger. I think that that can only go so far. You end up bitter and overwhelmed. I think that there is something beyond that. [Toronto, 2003]

Austin Clarke:
The Polished Hoe

Austin Clarke received the Giller Prize for his novel *The Polished Hoe* (2002). The novel also garnered a Commonwealth Writers Prize for Best Book as well as a Trillium Award for Ontario Book of the Year. Clarke has written nine previous novels, one of which, *The Origin of Waves* (1997) won the Rogers Writers' Trust Award. He has also produced several story collections and a handful of memoirs, including *Growing Up Stupid Under the Union Jack* (1980). Clarke, who came to Canada from Barbados in 1955, is a Member of the Order of Canada. He was honoured in 1999 with a W.O. Mitchell award for his extensive body of work and for his contributions to young writers. I have interviewed Clarke several times, first in 1997 for the *Globe and Mail*, when he was still living at the brownstone on McGill Street. It was in February, well past Christmas, but ornaments still adorned his home and he served me Christmas cake. He told me that he likes to extend the holiday season as long as possible. Clarke has moved since then to a street just north of mine. He remains one of my favourite interviews. He is a superb raconteur and he treats journalists as guests. If you show up anywhere near noon he will give you a glass of wine or a martini. The afternoon I met with him a few months ago, I asked for tea and we settled in for a nice chat.

Donna Bailey Nurse: Were you surprised to win the Giller?

Austin Clarke: When I was writing *The Polished Hoe* I felt that it could be a glorious book. But at the same time I felt that it could have failed because of all the experimentation that I was indulging in, because of the new ground I was breaking, which was to have a woman sitting down in a room with a man and talking for twenty-four hours. How was I going to sustain the interest? Although I am not a mystery writer, I am quite aware that you have got somehow to sustain a very high level of intensity. To do this for a substantial length of time is a feat. The other thing too that is important is the way I've used language in the speech, and the way I've used language in the discursive parts of the book.

DBN: I was fascinated by the use of childhood singing games and calypso music in the novel. What are you saying about the significance of the vernacular voice?

AC: I am saying that the vernacular is the lingua franca of Bimshire, of Barbados. I am also saying that one can no longer deprecate this language by calling it a dialect. Because if we West Indians consider ourselves to be a people, then certainly we have got to make a judgment on the language that the English colonizers spoke to us—and some of that language is unintelligible. It is not syntatically unintelligible, but it is unintelligible when spoken to us by those people. So why can't those people—the English colonizers—consider the question from our point of view?

DBN: In many ways *The Polished Hoe* reminds me of Toni Morrison's *Song of Solomon* which is a work that suggests the vernacular does more than express a culture, it embodies it.

AC: It is the lifeblood of a culture. I got this in a very strange way from Patrick Chamoiseau in his novel *Texaco*. I realized that he could not have written *Texaco* unless he had written a new language for his characters to speak. I tried to imitate it. I tried to make the people who inhabit Bimshire speak this language. Of course it is not purely Bimshire. It is a language comprised by Mary Mathilda from all the strange voices she heard in her dining room where Mr. Bellfeels brought his friends. She was able to retain some of the nuances of this language. So when she was speaking, particularly to Sargeant, she was reproducing what she heard as the language of Europe in Barbadian terms, and that qualified her to criticize other aspects of the civilization of Europe.

DBN: You admire Miles Davis so much, and a lot of times your writing reminds me of his playing. Is this intentional?

AC: You have done me a compliment. I wish that I had been able to infuse in my writing an aspect of Miles Davis's brilliance on the trumpet. I listened very attentively to Miles Davis when I was writing certain passages of *The Polished Hoe*. I think, without knowing music, I have been exposed to enough music to understand somewhat what he is attempting to achieve.

DBN: What draws you to Miles Davis?

AC: The sounds of his trumpet, the lyricism, the anger, the pacing, the universalist appeal. And equally, his disregard of the people to whom he is playing.

DBN: It's true that he doesn't care very much about the audience, but you do.

AC: I do. More than Miles Davis does.

DBN: Tell me in your own words, not what happens in the novel, but what the novel is about?

AC: The novel is a reminiscence of a woman who is narrating her experience, and the experience of her mother, which she is morally able to justify using as her experience, and the experience of her grandmother who was a slave. It is her history. It is also her future, because she is warning generations to come to be careful in any relationship they have to the plantation. They may not be in a position to determine the kind of relationship they are going to have to the plantation. But she is at least saying be careful about relationships you are swept into with the plantation.

It is a book about success. It is a book about negotiation. It is a book about improvisation. But most importantly it is about a book about a woman who is not a victim. She has been victimized, but she is not a victim because she has declared her pride and dignity and liberation in the act she commits and by her thoughts of repudiating Europe.

DBN: Why is victim such a bad word? It is not a shame to be a victim.

AC: It is not a shame to be a victim. But it is a condition of unwholesomeness to be regarded as a victim. We do not ascribe any feelings of compassion for the victim in this book because we feel the victim negotiates on her own an aspect of her victimhood. Mary Mathilda is actually helped by the plantation, the system. The system and the plantation means colonialism, and colonialism has been beneficial to some blacks. It has not been beneficial to most. I don't want Mary Mathilda to be perceived as a victim precisely because I feel that I succeeded in making her a woman who rose above these circumstances.

DBN: Why is this a Canadian novel?

AC: It is a Canadian novel because I say it is a Canadian novel. In Toronto today, March 25, 2003, there are enough Barbadians who can identify with the book and there are enough Canadians who, if they are willing, could identify with the book and be able to transfer the positions in the book from Barbados to Toronto. In Toronto there is a sizeable

Barbadian community. If I talk about Canada I've got to talk about Barbadians living in Canada and they are no longer Barbadians because they live in Canada. So Canada in its characteristics is Barbadian, as it is Trinidadian. It is a very narrow-minded, if not racist attitude, that says to me my book *The Polished Hoe* is a Barbadian book. It is Canadian.

DBN: Were you surprised at the sharp criticism the book received in some quarters?

AC: I'm not surprised at the reservations in certain quarters of the so-called literary establishment to *The Polished Hoe*.

DBN: Do you think it has to do with subject matter? Race is such a sensitive topic, it sometimes prevents critics from writing sensibly about it.

AC: There is the presumption that these people know about black writing or West Indian writing, or that they know about the writings by persons who were not born here of the white race. And I feel we cannot have an intellectual group in any society talking about black literature when the intellectual group in the same society does not know how to handle elements of racism.

DBN: In your interview with *Hot Type* you said that people who lack power must make accommodations. In other words, Mary Mathilda was forced to become Bellfeel's mistress in order to make the most of her life.

AC: Mary made tremendous accommodations. She gave up her dignity, a large slice of her pride, to accommodate Mr. Bellfeels. But this was not something of her own initiative. Her mother had told her from the beginning that if she decided not to be involved with Bellfeels there would be ten other women in the village who would do it. Her mother knew that Mary had the best qualifications for being Bellfeel's mistress. She was pretty and of the right complexion. This, to me, was a very pragmatic view of the situation.

DBN: How do you know so much about so many different things? When you are talking about Mary Mathilda walking down the road, you know what the road is made of; and when Mary Mathilda hears a sound, you recognize all the components of that sound; and when a character cooks a chicken you know precisely the method that's involved.

AC: It's instinct. I know so much because I love the situation, I love the geography of the place, I love the people inhabiting the place. I love the conditions of the inhabitants. So there is very little for me to do apart from observing. Even though I've lived abroad from Barbados, I am still able to recreate the Barbadian sensibility in the novel. And that comes from a longing to belong. And a serious passion for language. That's the only way I can explain it.

DBN: Tell me about the Barbados you remember.

AC: Well, the Barbados that I was born and raised in is beautiful, pastoral, green. We had land, which means we had sugar cane fields and goats and sheeps and pigs. So we had a very agricultural situation at home. Then I went to Harrison College in Bridgetown. It was very urban and sophisticated. I must comment on the tremendous education I got in Barbados that prepared me for living in this city. My upbringing in Barbados is responsible for my self-assurance in this country, in this city, after all these years. When I think about Barbados, I think about the most beautiful aspect of my life. Of going for moonlight walks with my friends to the factory where you would drink the crack liquor from the sugar cane. Things that you can't do in this city because this city is too urban. But I'm sure country children in Canada used to do indulge in these kinds of activities as well.

DBN: Are you a passionate reader?

AC: I would not say I am a passionate reader, but I do read every night.

DBN: Do you have a favourite novel?

AC: Not really.

DBN: I sometimes associate your work with the Victorians. Your memoir *Growing Up Stupid Under the Union Jack* reminds me of [Thomas Hughes']*Tom Brown's School Days*. And *The Polished Hoe* has an eerie Victorian feel.

AC: That's because I was brought up on the Victorians. Particularly Dickens. I consider Dickens to be a black man writing about Barbados. [Toronto, 2003]

Nalo Hopkinson:
Fantasy Island Girl

Nalo Hopkinson's first novel, *Brown Girl in the Ring* (1998), about a young black woman in a futuristic Toronto, netted her a Warner Aspect First Novel Prize. In the few short years since the publication of that novel, Hopkinson's distinct, womanist Caribbean-flavoured fantasies have pushed her to the forefront of the sci-fi community. Hopkinson's second novel, *Midnight Robber* (2000), was selected as a *New York Times* notable book of the year. A collection of stories, *Skin Folk*, appeared in 2001. Hopkinson is also the editor of two anthologies: *Whispers from the Cotton Tree Root: Caribbean Fabulist Fiction* (2002) and *Mojo: Conjure Stories* (2003). In 1999 she was awarded the John W. Campbell Award for Best New Writer. Hopkinson's third novel, *The Salt Roads*, will be released in the fall of 2003. Born in Jamaica in 1960, Hopkinson is the daughter of the late poet Slade Hopkinson, a founding member, along with Derek Walcott, of the Trinidad Theatre Workshop. She settled in Toronto in the mid-1970s. I invited her to my home for dinner, where we shared a meal of broiled salmon and herbed rice.

Donna Bailey Nurse: I heard that when you learned that the science fiction writer Samuel Delaney was black, you cried.

Nalo Hopkinson: Yes.

DBN: What was it? Permission to write?

NH: It was company. My universe had just doubled in size. I knew all kinds of black writers. I didn't know any black science fiction writers or readers. So this man, whose work was doing things to me that I could not even describe, was a black man.

DBN: Is this when you really started writing?

NH: At this point I was writing health articles for *Word* magazine... I went into HMV to buy music for my fitness class and there was this black urban magazine. I picked it up and I liked it and I emailed them and said this is wonderful. The editor, Phil Vassell, said, "Would you like to write for me?" I'd never thought of doing it.

The thing to understand is that I was often not aware of my own thought processes. I grew up not thinking about that much. Yes, I can remember reading some fantasy novels and looking at the folklore on which it was based and thinking, We have folklore. And every so often thinking that a sentence would be better if...but I would close these thoughts down. It's that thing we were talking about earlier. The big problem often for black women writing is daring to think you can think about doing it. That was definitely part of it. Definitely part of it was me trying to fit in, me trying to do what was expected of me, or trying to understand where there was room for me. The world wasn't reflecting me back to myself. To see Whoopi Goldberg in *Jumpin' Jack Flash*. It was the first time and the last time I've seeing a freaky black woman large as life and twice as African who is also a computer geek, has dreads, gets the guy and doesn't die.

DBN: People are really resistant to accepting the full humanity of black women.

NH: I felt there was no room for me in the world...so I was very, very tired. There almost wasn't any point hoping for stuff because you weren't going to get it anyway. But there was the author Judy Merrill offering this course at Ryerson. I knew Judy wasn't very well. And I didn't how much longer she would be teaching. This was my only chance to get into the course. She wanted people who were writing at about the same level of competence. So you had to send her some of your fiction, which assumed that you had been writing fiction...so, here I am now, 30 years old, trying to write science fiction because Judy Merrill wants to see some writing. I'd written a piece before for the *Word* on health risks particular to black people. I came across research that had been done in the U.K. where they had discovered that levels of schizophrenia amongst Caribbean men in the U.K. were higher than in any other population. They were trying to figure out what that was. And they figured it was about losing social support. I thought it was fascinating. That's what *Brown Girl in the Ring* started from. At first I made the character delusional. I wrote six pages and had no idea what to do with it. Just sent it to Judy. I got into the class, and the class never ran. But she encouraged us to start our own writing group.

DBN: You had such an easy time getting *Brown Girl in the Ring* published. It hardly seems fair, does it?

NH: People ask: "How hard was it to to get published? How often have you been rejected?" Well I have been rejected. But I also kept realistic. When I first started writing I had learned to put a sentence together. I was in a comfort zone and then I stretched a little bit. *Brown Girl* did happen very quickly. But the part where it was little bit by little bit, no one saw that. It was just like: "Here I am."

DBN: Could you quickly go over the story behind *Brown Girl in the Ring*?

NH: I had these pages and I didn't know what to do so I put them aside. I could feel the work needed to be a novel and that was very frightening. So I put it away to work on a short story. You tend to get published first as a short story writer anyway. You work on a novel anywhere from a year to ten years and usually it sucks and you start all over again. A short story can take anywhere from a day to a year and then you start all over again. So I worked at short stories.

DBN: "A Habit of Waste"?

NH: "A Habit of Waste" got written with my writing group. I couldn't make a story happen. I couldn't do beginning, middle, end. "A Habit of Waste" is perhaps the first time where I successfully did that. And I did it by putting two completely different things together—a technique I still use now.

DBN: What two things did you put together?

NH: One thing was this idea I'd always had. There are so many homeless people in Toronto and so many hungry people in Toronto, and I look around and the city is full of food. Not just food you have to pay for. There are trees growing and there is game. You could probably feed off the land in the middle of this city. Then I took a quote from my Dad's poem, which is one of his best known ["Madwoman of Papine: Two Cartoons with Captions"]. On the face of it they have nothing to do with each other. I crunched them together and the energy of trying to make them fit...created a story.

DBN: "A Habit of Waste" is the story where the main character, a black woman, switches to a white body.

NH: Yes. I still struggle all the time with body image. And I was having a bad body day: I was feeling really fat. I was feeling like I let myself go. I saw somebody getting on the streetcar who looked like I used to look....

I just didn't appreciate it. I used to think even then I was really fat. I got into work in this horrible mood and said to one of my co-workers, I just saw someone getting on the streetcar with the body I used to have. And she said, "That sounds like one of your stories." I didn't do any work that day. People ask where you get your ideas and it's never one thing. The article I read in *OMNI* a decade before and the poem of my dad. And a woman with a nice butt getting on the streetcar. All of these came together in "A Habit of Waste."

DBN: Every science fiction writer seems to have a very specific definition of their work. I want you to define for me, if you can, what you are doing.

NH: I am interested in science fiction and fantasy. Those are the literatures that interest me. That's what I read. I tend not to read more of what I would call mimetic fiction or fiction that is imitating reality. And I guess that's because I grew up so depressed and so much mimetic fiction feels like more depression to me. Life sucks and then you die. I guess I'm being very unfair.

DBN: You are. I think a lot of English literature is pretty fantastical. Certainly Dickens.

NH: Yes that's right. Life sucks and then you die.

DBN: No, you don't die in the end. You never die in the end. That's the whole thing. It's all a musical.

NH: Yes. But your friends die. Your wife is sick. Your kids die. You're poor.

DBN: But how is your writing happier than that?

NH: I am being very facetious. In the fantastical genres there is an idea that the world can change. And that to me is immensely hopeful. I got into a mild argument with a colleague at a party a few weeks ago. She's dealing with men who read a lot of porno who become estranged from their wives. And she's trying to find models in folklore for positive ways to look at women. I was saying to her, You can't replace sexual excitement with fairy tales. What you are doing is demonizing porn. I won't get into arguments about porn versus erotica, because erotic material or explicitly sexual material is something I write, it's something I read, it's something I enjoy and I'm able to maintain connections with people. She said, I understand what you are saying but I don't have a radical agenda here.

And I said, Alright, but I gotta tell you that for me to exist in this world I have to have a radical agenda because the world has got to change in order for people like me to be able to exist.

DBN: That's right. White writers have themes. Black writers have agendas.

NH: Well I'm owning it. I need to have a radical agenda. I need to make a world where it is perfectly okay that I'm attracted to people who live in between genders. I think that should not be a problem. I can't change. The world has to change.

DBN: You do begin to realize that the world is freaky. The world is science fiction. In fact, has William Gibson not just written a novel that is set in present time even though it is science fiction?

NH: We are the future.

DBN: If the future is now, what is the future of science fiction?

NH: This is a question that science fiction writers are kind of huddling together and asking themselves in scared voices. I'm not worried about it. I think we'll figure it out as we go along. I have colleagues who are also being told, "What you're writing is not science fiction." And yet they can't get published in the mainstream because the mainstream is saying, Oh that's too weird. There's a slippage happening.

DBN: That's true because we're sort of behind, in mimetic fiction as you put it. . . .

NH: It's starting to feel historical.

DBN: Yes, it is. Even though I like it.

NH: In that kind of fiction you'll be lucky if a cellphone shows up. Whereas I was walking through the airport the other day and there was a guy with a thing in his ear. It was blue and the blue light was flashing and that was his phone.

DBN: That's like in *Midnight Robber*.

NH: But you won't see that in many fiction novels, and if you do, they're going to call it science fiction.

DBN: You know where I noticed this historical slippage? In reading Zadie Smith's *The Autograph Man*. In that novel anyone who is not a Chinese Jew or a Black Jew feels very marginal. Christianity is marginal. But once you recognize London as racially diverse how can you go back and write a novel where the vast majority of Londoners are white?

NH: Walter Mosley says that science fiction is a literature that says the world can change. And it's a literature that says that as a black writer you can have as wide and varied a palate as you want. LeVar Burton has a science fiction novel out. Did you know that? I don't find the novel terribly strong. But the premise, I adore. A black man becomes president of the USA.

DBN: That is science fiction.

NH: That's page one. Page two, he's assassinated.

DBN: But, really, what makes that premise science fiction?

NH: It is futuristic because that's not happening tomorrow. Octavia Butler says she writes cautionary literature. But most science fiction writers claim that's not what they are doing. Octavia Butler says people need to pay attention. If we keep doing that shit we'll be in shit.

DBN: You do a bit of that, don't you think?

NH: It's hard because I want to write stories that have people dying to turn the page. But I also have things that get on my nerves that I want to talk about. The story has to happen first. And you are always doing this juggle. And there are stories I have abandoned because they were rants. Yet I believe that people have to be able to rant.

DBN: Your stories come across as cautionary once in a while because they often point out what we've let go of. We've let go of craftsmanship. Hard labour is good for the soul, you seem to be saying sometimes. What really thrilled me with the first novel is that after the economy crashes people begin to barter again. How exciting.

NH: I wasn't so much saying that hard labour is good for the soul, because I'm no lover of hard labour. But the fact that it happens, as well as the fact that people find ways to get around it is important. When people ask me to define science fiction and fantasy I say they are the literatures that explore the fact that we are toolmakers and users, and are always changing our environment. The tool might be a toaster oven. It might be figuring out that if you take clay from a certain part of the riverbed and put it in the fire it hardens and you can now store water in it. It might be a religion. Although people aren't going to be very happy to think of religion as something you make.

DBN: You sometimes talk about what kind of technologies African peoples might have come up with if they had had the chance. In *Midnight Robber* you introduce AI—artificial intelligence. Why have you imagined this particular technology for this particular people?

NH: I have to give props to Uppinder Mehan. He's from Toronto. South Asian. He wrote a piece about continental Indian science fiction writers and the difficulties they face in doing the kind of extrapolation that is so much part of science fiction. I find this problem too. People make all kinds of assumptions. They'll assume that I'm just repeating folklore. They won't see the extrapolations because they don't know them. But one of the things Uppinder said that really got me thinking was that before the western world spread its technology worldwide, other cultures were developing their own metaphors for technologies and their own technologies. That's kind of where *Midnight Robber* came from.

The metaphors we use in the west come from Greek and European mythology. Aishu in West African religious mythology is the deity I use in *Midnight Robber*. Aishu said: "I would like to go everywhere and see everything," a perfect metaphor for artificial intelligence. Black people have a rich spiritual heritage, as well as a rich imaginative life—stories handed down over centuries—that inform our ideas of the future. They need to be on the table like everybody else's. [Toronto, 2003]

Andre Alexis, Nalo Hopkinson and Djanet Sears:

Black Writers on Being Edited, Published and Reviewed in Canada

What does is mean to be a "black writer" in Canada? How does race affect the writer-editor relationship? Should the racial background of a writer be taken into consideration when marketing and selling a book? I sat down with fiction writer Andre Alexis, science fiction writer Nalo Hopkinson and playwright Djanet Sears to discuss these issues, and others, over a West Indian meal of rice and peas, plantain, jerk chicken and curry goat in the offices of *Quill & Quire*. ("Rice and peas at *Quill & Quire*!"Alexis noted with some amazement.)

Donna Bailey Nurse: Do you define yourselves as black writers?

Andre Alexis: For me, this is a very complicated issue. When you used the word black it doesn't have one meaning. Every time I speak to someone who uses the world black it usually involves a discussion of trying to figure out what they mean by it, and if they are trying to indicate me. I think the most frustrating thing is that you have to discuss it.

Djanet Sears: One of the interesting questions for me is: Are our readers black? Who buys our work? Are most of them black? Where are the patrons of the black arts?

Nalo Hopkinson: I'm sure they are there. Because even though the field of science fiction is largely white, I worked for a while at Bakka Books [a science fiction bookstore in Toronto] and a lot of the people coming into the store were not white. They were not coming to the conventions, they were not part of the sci-fi community events I go to. But they are as much my readers as anybody else.

DBN: Do you think that black authors are, or should be, marketed any differently?

NH: I have no basis of comparison: I've only ever been black! [Laughter] To some extent I am involved in the discussion about marketing with my publisher and I'm gathering that this may be rare. And I think it might be because I'm one of fewer than ten black writers in my field and because I have a publisher who is very interested in trying to right that imbalance and so she is going out and looking for other markets.

DBN: Do you feel she needs to do that?

NH: To some extent. For instance, by putting a black person on the cover of *Brown Girl in the Ring*, I think she went way further than many publishers do.

AA: When *Childhood* was first published in Canada, it was with McClelland & Stewart. It had a picture on the cover that was as racially neutral as you can imagine—a butterfly. I liked that image. That was sensitive to me, because as you read the novel you don't find out that a person is of a particular colour until thirty pages in. And that was done on purpose. They put a black child on the cover of the British edition. I told them that the race of the child was supposed to be a bit of a surprise and that you are supposed to identify, whoever you are, with this voice. They went with the image anyway. I don't know whether they felt black kids are popular with British people in general or whether they thought it would attract more black British people to the novel.

DBN: Djanet, your play *Harlem Duet* tells the story of a black man who leaves his wife for a white woman. Did you worry about the fact that white audiences might not like the racial content? Did you worry about how it would be marketed?

DS: As a writer I am this very self-absorbed person who is writing a story that I would like. And then it's time to give it out and I want people to like it and I want people to come and see it performed. But I set up a very harsh world. I ask what five hundred years of white supremacy has done to the black psyche. So, to answer your question: I do think about what people will like, but I think about it way too late. In terms of promoting the play, I found there are biases in terms of what people think when they see two black actors on a poster and the title is *Harlem Duet*. Some audience members phoned to say they thought it was a musical. So what do images of black people tell the majority of consumers about black people?

DBN: Does it matter who reviews your work?

AA: Not even a little bit. You just want someone who is attuned to whatever sensibility you have.

DBN: When the movie version of Toni Morrison's *Beloved* was released there were virtually no black Canadian critics discussing the movie in the mainstream press. Is that okay?

AA: I don't know if it would be okay for Toni Morrison, but it would be all right for me.

DS: Nine times out of ten, I do prefer black reviewers. They will have the knowledge of some of the references that I use as a springboard for my pieces. But, then again, when I was working with Noel Baker—a white guy—at the Canadian Film Centre, he knew all my references. But he's enormously well-read.

NH: It's very important to me that the reviewer recognize the references I am using because I am drawing from a lot of places. It would matter to me if no black people or no Caribbean people were reviewing my work. It would bother me if nobody from the contexts important to me—and I occupy five or six different spaces—were reviewing my work. Then I'd have a problem.

DS: I'm trying to pull at the weeds of race. If the reader doesn't understand this as a dramatic or a emotional difficulty, they won't read the piece as dramatic or emotional. They will read the piece as more of a political or ideological rant.

DBN: Which is what happened at the *Globe and Mail* when Kate Taylor reviewed your play.

DS: Well, she did spend much of her time talking about the white woman who only appears as a hand through a door. The story's not about that character. But since there is no principal white character in the play, Kate Taylor didn't see herself in the story, and she wasn't able to enter the soul of the play through the hearts of the black characters. Black people often have the opposite experience. When we see Tarzan, we enter the story through Tarzan and don't relate to the Africans. Yes, people need to see themselves, but white audiences get to see themselves in stories all the time. They need to open themselves up to the other facets of the human experience. Unfortunately Kate Taylor probably saw herself in *Harlem Duet* as just a hand. It probably hurt her a lot—not being at the centre of the story; and she took it as a real slight. I think that's the point of view she took.

AA: This brings up a very important issue to me. A very important part of what makes me human is speculating about whether God is there; speculating about belonging; speculating about how the imagination changes the place that you occupy. I am absolutely a writer of colour. That's who I am. But I really want to insist that I have the right to speculate on things that aren't directly to do with race. I prefer that you don't read my book and look at it as the product of a black person. I would prefer that you take it and look at it as speculation about faith, about God, about place.

DBN: As a black critic I want people to see that blackness is everything. That is why I continually throw the term out there, because I want people—especially black people—to see that the term black has the same complexity as the term white.

AA: But when somebody says this is a "black book" it feels like an effort to pigeonhole something that has taken you years to do. It puts you in such a weird position in which you have to assert that you are something when people say you are not and assert you're not something when people say you are, just so you can have some middle ground.

DBN: Does race figure into the editing process? Are the right questions asked?

DS: Playwrights work with dramaturges. With the last piece I had two main dramturges who worked simultaneously. I used Kate Lushington and Diane Roberts, a white woman and a black woman. Sometimes they didn't agree, and I liked that because it reflected some of the difficulties I wanted to explore in the play.

AA: Editing is being in a very tight situation with someone whose judgment and whose intellectual and emotional honesty you trust. You have to bounce [the work] off someone. You're searching for a person who is honest. Who will tell you what they think and not what you want to hear. At some level this is an area where race can't enter. If you're suggesting that race is the sense of bias, that's unhelpful for the work itself. You want an emotional receptor. If it's a white emotional receptor that's fine. But if Ellen Seligman's main value to me was her race then

I think she would be less valuable to my work. It's not about asking the right questions but about whether you ask a consistent set of questions so that I know where you're coming from. This is where I would be really cautious about race coming into it, because it would seem to put its emphasis on something outside the writing.

DS: That's only true if the work has nothing to do with race. I believe that everyone comes with a bias based on the matrix of their experience. So I have to find a way to create a mirror. Especially in a play dealing with race, I need people who understand, but there are different ways of understanding. Both Kate and Diane are good friends of mine but they have different experiences surrounding race. Kate is white, Jewish and from England. Diane is black Canadian and of Caribbean ancestry. Their responses help me to gauge the audience. It isn't because one is black and will understand where I'm coming from and one is white and so won't understand where I'm coming from. They are both friends of mine. They both understand where I am coming from.

NH: That is why I would never want to go with one editor. I need a whole lot of different perspectives because I am trying to bridge so many different things. It is helpful to have an editor who knows where I am coming from and it is helpful for me to have an editor who doesn't.

DBN: In the end, does it make a difference that you are working in an extremely white environment?

DS: When we talk about white culture sometimes we generalize. We are actually talking about the gatekeepers who tend to have one face. It's the gatekeepers I'm often challenging. I'm not talking about the people who come to my shows. I'm not talking about my friends. I'm talking about the editors at newspapers, the producers at the television stations. Who do they hire and why do they hire who they do?

AA: Even the gatekeepers are not monolithic. I'm thinking of Avie Bennett, head of McClelland & Stewart. I'm talking about a Jewish man with a good sense of humour who has been extremely kind to me and so doesn't at all correspond to a notion of exclusivity I might have had if I had not met him.

NH: Sometimes when I scratch at the surface that looks mostly white I'm quite surprised by what I see. White culture is not monolithic and black culture is not monolithic. You learn to find your allies. [*Quill & Quire*, 2000]

Reviews

The Worlds Within Her

by Neil Bissoondath
Knopf Canada, 417 pages

A ny day now the winners of the 1999 Governor General's Awards will be announced. Among the nominees for the highly coveted fiction prize is acclaimed Trinidadian born author, Neil Bissoondath. His novel, *The Worlds Within Her*, is the story of a woman who returns to her Caribbean birthplace and is forced to confront her family's past. Bissoondath is something of a controversial figure in literary circles, for his writing (especially *Selling Illusions: The Cult of Multiculturalism in Canada*, 1994) often criticizes the notion of group identity.

I must declare up front that Bissoondath's politics do not sit well with me. I mention this only because his views are so central to his novel and because his characters are frequently reduced to mouthpieces for his positions. In spite of this, *The Worlds Within Her* is a well-written, quietly absorbing tale.

Yasmin Summerhayes, an aloof, 40-something anchorwoman of Hindu heritage living in Canada, is taking her dead mother's ashes back to Trinidad. The visit promises an opportunity for Yasmin to learn more about her family's history, especially about her father, a respected Indian activist who was assassinated when she was small.

But Yasmin is reticent about the visit. She feels no links to the land of her birth and no ties whatsoever to her Indian roots. On the other hand, a holiday will at least put some distance between Yasmin and her husband, Jim, who have been growing apart since the death of their child.

When Yasmin arrives on the island, the people are still recovering from a violent coup attempt. It is a land stymied by economic hardship that continues to play out long-standing tensions between its Indian and African population. Nevertheless, Yasmin is moved by the beauty around her, particularly the view from the family estate that is home to her father's brother, sister, cousin and maid.

The Worlds Within Her actually tells three separate stories: The first charts the history of Yasmin and Jim's relationship; the second chronicles Yasmin's parents' unfulfilling marriage.

In the third story Yasmin's relatives resurrect memories of her father's turbulent political career. The novel spins like a musical round. One story begins, then the second joins in and finally the third. Round and round it goes until the entire tale unwinds. It is a fragmented and unnecessarily complicated way to tell a story, but you get used to it after a while.

All the characters in the book are engaging. There's Penny, Yasmin's bitter spinster aunt and Cyril, her father's kind brother. And there is Amina, the taciturn family helper who seems as old as the island itself. The most fascinating personality of all belongs to Yasmin's mother Shakti, an intelligent amusing woman who has adopted the mannerisms of the upper-class British society she adores. Shakti spends her days drinking English tea and reminiscing about her marriage. Unfortunately, Shakti placed a distant second in her husband's affections. Vernon "Ram" Ramessar's first love was politics. He devoted his entire life to improving conditions for the Indian people. But Shakti describes Ram as a grasping untrustworthy figure, willing to neglect his family and manipulate his followers to achieve political objectives.

Through the character of Ram, we are encouraged to question the idea of "a people" with a common history. Bissoondath presents the notion of collective memory as completely fraudulent and dangerous. Indeed Ram's politics lead to his assassination.

Other rebellious Indian figures, such as cousin Ash, are proven pathetic, and even Uncle Cyril exposes a vicious side when he speaks of Indians protecting themselves from "black boys."

The political and racial strife exists within a context of British imperialism and white privilege, although this is a point Bissoondath fails to highlight. The island's British inhabitants are as invisible and omnipresent as the air. Oddly Bissoondath does not portray them as possessing a strong sense of identity. Indeed some of the book's white characters seem oblivious to such ideas. When Shakti asks Jim where his people are from, he must stop to consider what she means.

While identifying with the group leads Bissoondath's Indian characters to racism and violence, such identification is presented as a redeemable character flaw in the makeup of white people. Yasmin comes to accept her mother-in-law's boycott of her wedding ceremony as a symptom of mere social discomfort. Bissoondath repeatedly depicts white racism as a simple case of bad manners.

Certainly his argument contains an element of truth. Many acts of racism may indeed be construed as instances of extreme bad manners. But sometimes Bissoondath writes dishonestly about race, as in the scene where Yasmin explains to her daughter that white women sunbathe in order to become brown. When the child retorts that she wishes she were white, Yasmin thinks "Why was it acceptable for that woman to dream of being brown, but not so for her daughter to dream of being white?" Does Bissoondath really believe that wanting to have a tan is exactly the same thing as wanting to belong to a dark-skinned race? The suggestion insults our intelligence.

In *The Worlds Within Her* Bissoondath goes to great lengths to invalidate the idea of collective memory and collective history. Bissoondath's work conveys his concern that, taken to the extreme, group identification can result in ugly nationalistic violence and certainly, any casual stroll through history will confirm his fears. At the same time his dismissal of collective experience is an unusual enough stance for a storyteller. From time immemorial people have told stories in order to *instill* a sense of group identity. Stories transmit history, strengthen community bonds, celebrate tradition and create a sense of belonging. Stories help human beings ward off their sense of loneliness in the world. They remind us of our connections to one another. However, there are certain connections Bissoondath deems superfluous. In *The Worlds Within Her* Shakti never tells Yasmin the story of her dead father because she fears "he would remain just a construction. I do not want Yasmin to have to live with that disappointment."

Perhaps Bissoondath is simply posing rhetorical questions. Was Shakti right to deny Yasmin information about her father just because her memory was imperfect? Should people of colour forget about their ancestors just because their ancestors are dead? If we agree to forget our history, are Europeans prepared to relinquish theirs too? [*Pride*, 1999]

Doing The Heart Good
by Neil Bissoondath
Cormorant, 328 pages

Quebec City writer Neil Bissoondath has published a number of memorable novels including *The Worlds Within Her* and *A Casual Brutality* (1989), yet people tend to identify him primarily with his out-spoken views about multiculturalism. In short, he believes that official multiculturalism actually discourages Canadian unity by promoting ethnic differences. Although what seems to disturb Bissoondath most about the policy is that it lures Canadians away from the dominant British heritage.

The great irony of this is that Bissoondath's feelings are likely the bitter by-product of his own ethnicity, the deeply ingrained lessons of his West Indian heritage. It is a unique West Indian who emerges culturally unscathed from that particularly soul-destroying brand of racism known as the Caribbean colonial system. One thing little brown children are taught to believe in is the superiority of the English. And since everything you worship or read either ignores your existence or figures you in the most unappealing light, you really can't help but come to accept your heritage as inferior.

The Quebec context of Bissoondath's latest novel transforms this anglophilia from an issue of race to one of language. In *Doing the Heart Good*, Bissoondath grapples with English's embattled status in Quebec. One of the main things his story insists upon—as if there were some lingering doubt—is that English-speaking people value their language as well and deeply as do the French.

Much to my chagrin, his views do not seem to prevent him from being an elegant and accomplished writer. *Doing the Heart Good* may well be recognized as his finest book yet. It draws us into warm acquaintance with Alistair Mackenzie, a kind yet stubborn Second World War veteran. Alistair's memories of his life (he was born at the end of the First World War) chart the social tensions, especially the linguistic tensions, of twentieth-century Montreal.

When we meet Alistair he has lost his home in a fire and has been living with his daughter's family. He escapes the flames with his most prized possessions, his precious war medals, which symbolize his identity as a loyal subject of the British crown.

The war left Alistair with a limp and severely damaged hearing. He harbours a quiet disdain for those who had the opportunity to fight, and like his neighbour Tremblay, did not. This tension between the francophone Tremblay and the anglo Alistair encapsulates the French-English strife at the heart of the novel.

The conflict is managed with wonderful deftness. We hear about the city's various social issues as they light a path through Alistair's life, for one of the points Bissoondath likes to make is that history should be more of a personal preoccupation than a national one.

Memories of his own outrage during the FLQ crisis start a terrific row between Alistair and his francophone son-in-law Jacques (whom he insists on calling Jack). At another point he recalls the accusations of racism that shut down Sir George Williams University in 1969. And the death of his beloved wife Mary, occurring the year before the murders of the fourteen female students at the L'Ecole Polytechnique, will forever be linked in his memory to that sad event.

Alistair is a retired professor from Concordia University (where Bissoondath taught in the 1990s—today he teaches at Laval), a specialist in nineteenth-century English literature and a passionate fan of Dickens. For Alistair, Dickens is the English language made sublime, a symbol of the culture he would like to pass along to his married daughter. His daughter, however, has not only married a francophone, she is raising a son who does not speak a word of English.

If Alistair has a favourite Dickens book it is *A Tale of Two Cities*, a title with particular resonance for this novel. Themes the novel evokes and the atmosphere created are like a contemporary reworking of the ideas in Hugh MacLennan's *Two Solitudes*.

Bissoondath has written his story with Dickens in mind. It is a satisfying, old-fashioned read, filled with social commentary, physical comedy and Alistair's memories of a diverse cast of unforgettable people.

Like Dickens's *A Christmas Carol* the plot unfolds over Christmas Eve and Christmas Day, and as in that novel our hero spends his time combing through his memories to recall the people who have done his heart good. Chief among them is his wife, Mary, whom he married after the war. She is a figure directly out of a 1940s Myrna Loy film and one of the liveliest females to grace the pages of Canadian literature.

And this novel itself is lively. It will cause you, at points, to break into side-splitting laughter. I enjoyed it so much that I can't resist giving away a bit of the ending. It is a scene that perhaps only a loyal British subject like Alistair or Bissoondath (or I) could love. It features Alistair's now bi-cultural family gathered round the Christmas turkey, a scene much like the one that concludes *A Christmas Carol*. We can almost hear Tiny Tim whisper: "God bless us everyone." (*The Gazette*, 2002)

In Another Place, Not Here
by Dionne Brand
Knopf Canada, 247 pages

F or many, the writings of Dionne Brand represent a conundrum. Readers often find it difficult to reconcile her strident prose denunciations of the status quo with the majestic pathos of her poetry. Brand's 1990 book-length poem, *No Language is Neutral*, garnered a Governor General's Award nomination, while a number of critics rejected her collection of essays *Bread Out of Stone* (1994) as vitriolic. In reality, all of Brand's creative endeavours—the short stories, essays, poetry and films—reveal her allegiance to the cause of social liberation, particularly the uplifting of black women.

Her debut novel, *In Another Place, Not Here*, chronicles the lives of two Caribbean women, Elizete, a poor cane worker, and Verlia, a lesbian and radical socialist, who fall in love during a revolution on an unnamed island, some time during the 1980s. The novel has echoes of works by Brand's African-American peers, particularly Alice Walker and *The Color Purple*.

Like that book's heroine, Celie, Elizete becomes the sexual property of a brutish man while still an adolescent. For a time, Elizete dreams of running away, but eventually she concludes: "Who is me to think I is something. I born to clean Isaiah's house and work cane since I was a child and all I have to do is lay down under him in the night and work the cane in the day."

Verlia also grows up in the Caribbean, but she belongs to a large, doting family and can afford to attend school regularly. When she turns 17, her family sends her to live with relatives in Sudbury, Ontario. Soon afterward, she flees to Toronto, where she becomes a socialist and immerses herself in the city's black power movement—much like the young Dionne Brand. Eventually, Verlia returns to the Caribbean where she joins the island's revolutionary effort.

Brand's mesmerizing voice lures the reader through a plot that oscillates between past and present. Her rendering of the island's slave history is sublimely evocative, and she transforms island patois into a kind of heroic poetry. Much of her narrative dealing with Toronto, however, seems pedestrian. As in past works, poetry emerges as Brand's first language and prose an uneasy second. *In Another Place, Not Here* suggests that history renders black women generally ineffectual. Despite that rather unfashionable sentiment, the novel reinforces Brand's status as a significant voice for the Caribbean-Canadian experience. [*Maclean's*, 1996]

At the Full and Change of the Moon

by Dionne Brand
Knopf Canada, 302 pages

"**S**o many stories waiting to be told"—the trite lyrics to some old song. Trite, maybe, but true. Stories *are* waiting to be told. They are patient, tenacious, as are memories, and just because nobody wants to hear them or just because nobody wants to remember, doesn't mean they're not out there. The stories of black people, for instance, are notoriously unpopular. But even black stories, sometimes, will out. If they come upon their ideal form and their true language, or if they can weasel their way into an eloquent voice, unwanted stories can become magically irresistible. So it was with *Song of Solomon* that waited for Toni Morrison, and so it was with *Crossing the River* that waited for Caryl Phillips and so it is now with *At the Full and Change of the Moon* that has waited for Dionne Brand.

At the Full and Change of the Moon is a novel comprised of intimately linked stories that chronicle the lives of a Trinidadian slave, Marie Ursule, and her descendants. The story spans several generations from the mid-nineteenth to late twentieth century and traverses the globe from India and the Caribbean to Europe and the Americas. A number of Brand's superbly delineated characters are strong enough to sustain entire novels of their own, especially Marie Ursule, who heads a secret organization of militant slaves known as *Sans Peur*. We meet Marie Ursule on Christmas Eve 1824, the very day her fellow bondsmen execute a mass suicide, an act of defiance calculated to bring their master to ruin. All the same, Marie Ursule cannot bear to end the life of her daughter, Bola, so she sends the child away in the care of Kamena, an escaped slave.

Brand draws us into a fierce, incendiary plantation world, a lush, dense revolutionary zone defined as much by insurrections and enclaves of escaped slaves as by its vast European plantations. Of course perspective is everything and this is a world seen through the senses of an African slave. The language of this section reflects the African experience and some readers will find Brand's complex lyricism difficult to stay with. But it would be particularly unfortunate for anyone to miss Kamena's sensual rendering of island cartography.

Kamena carries Bola to safety at desolate Culebra Bay. There, the spirit of Marie Ursule awakens the ghosts of two old nuns who raise Bola until she is old enough to care for herself. Bola grows up isolated, an eccentric creature of the bay. But she has scores of children with lonely men who pass through the inlet. Some of the children she sends away, some linger and essentially raise themselves, for Bola is too peculiar to be much of a mother to anyone.

At times *At the Full and Change of the Moon* seems to be carrying on a conversation with Toni Morrison's *Beloved*. As in *Beloved*, memories of people and places become suddenly concrete and intrude into contemporary time. And like *Beloved*, *At the Full and Change of the Moon* gives prominence to powerful ghosts.

However, *Beloved*, like most traditional African-American histories, is an "up from slavery" account. It marks a black woman's personal growth and evolution through the horror of her slave experience. Slavery in Brand's world is a sort of high point, a period during which dark-skinned peoples harboured certain goals and a fierce, unwavering pride. Manumission, on the other hand, brings about a steady deterioration of purpose, meaning and collective identity. The end of slavery initiates an epoch of self-inflicted injuries and betrayals.

As a youngster, Bola's grandson Samuel Sones befriends a wealthy white boy, embracing his new companion's books and dreams. He "had it in his mind to disappear into the English countryside with a milk-white woman. To stand like a man who was on the edge of a book page, overlooking a field and a milk-white woman." But when Samuel winds up in the English army during the First World War, he and the other black officers receive zero respect. He is eventually dishonourably discharged and returned to Trinidad. He spends his remaining days under the bitter tamarind tree, shamed into insanity by his own wrongheadedness.

In years to come, in the streets of America, one of Bola's descendants will sell narcotics, while in Amsterdam another will sell herself. In Toronto, another two descendants will abandon their offspring. These are characters who strive to obliterate their pasts, even when they possess little to replace their memories with. And this imperative to relinquish one's history, even when the act leaves one empty and disconnected, strikes me as profoundly sad and uniquely black Canadian.

Brand's most enduring figures are those who manage to remain linked to their own stories. Characters like Bola, the younger, who maintains a close relationship with her (grand)mother, even after the woman's death, and Marie Ursule, who creates a safe haven for her child by resurrecting the ghost nuns. These characters are in fact very much like Brand herself, who, through the sheer force of her imagination, wills an obscured history back to life. [*The Gazette*, 1999]

Eyeing the North Star: Directions in African Canadian Literature
Edited by George Elliott Clarke
McClelland & Stewart, 268 pages

Nova Scotian poet George Elliott Clarke's new anthology of short fiction and poetry reveals a native literature coming into its own. *Eyeing the North Star: Directions in African Canadian Literature* features the contemporary works of twenty-one black and Caribbean-Canadian authors. For the most part, the collection maintains a pleasing evenness of calibre, and largely forgoes the tiresome buddy system in which a small group of literary comrades takes turns anthologizing each other's work.

Twenty years ago Austin Clarke was the only black Canadian writer of global stature appearing in such collections. *Eyeing the North Star* boasts the works of many others of national and international renown, including Dany Laferrière, Olive Senior, Dionne Brand and Cecil Foster. In the introduction, the editor quotes author Andre Alexis, who longs for a "black Canadian writing that is conscious of Canada, writing that speaks not just about situation or about the earth, but from the earth." In fact, Clarke's own poems, including "Look Homeward, Exile," "Hymn to Portia White" and "The River Pilgrim: A Letter" emphatically satisfy Alexis's demand. Clarke's writing elaborates his singular "Africadian" sensibility—a blend of romanticized American slave/black loyalist/African-Canadian images that melt into a sensualized Maritime setting.

In the book's introduction, Clarke sets out to defend and define a tradition of black Canadian literature, just as he does in his last anthology, *Fire on the Water: An Anthology of Black Nova Scotian Writing* (1991). In his broad, seductive, loquacious argument, Clarke tends to weaken his declared purpose by emphasizing the diversity of styles found within the literature. At the same time he denies the primacy of racial politics: "Like Canada itself," he explains, "the African-Canadian 'community' fissures along regional, linguistic, gender, class and ethnic lines, thus rendering the incarnation of race solidarity a difficult enterprise. Thus, race, per se, is not everything for African-Canadians."

This rather obvious sentiment obscures the reality that few black writers anywhere in the world perceive race as "everything." They simply recognize, through their choice of subject matter and/or style, the inescapable significance of race in their experience.

In *Eyeing the North Star*, Olive Senior's poignant poem "All Clear, 1928" elaborates how shade bias within the community devastatingly impacts upon one Jamaican woman. Race also factors into Senior's technique. As in Pamela Mordecai's patois rendition of Christ's crucifixion, Senior's narrator employs an expressive West Indian vernacular, rather than standard English.

Racial history figures in a scene excerpted from Diana Braithwaite's one-act play *Martha and Elvira*, in which two former slave women exchange memories of bondage. The title of Makeda Silvera's short story, "No Beating Like Dis One," with its delineation of the acts of violence perpetrated against children in the name of discipline, also cleverly evokes the omnipresence of slave history.

If only by omission, race continues to influence Paul Tiyambe Zeleza in *The Rocking Chair*, a magic-realist account of an old man's loneliness; and Andre Alexis in the darkly absurdist fairy tales contained in *Despair: And Other Stories*. African-Canadian writers must make a conscious choice whether or not to enter a mainstream discourse which would refer to black characters as "other." Only three entirely new works appear in this collection, Cecil Foster's short story "The Rum," David Odhiambo's fiction poem "LIP" and a poem by Pamela Mordecai, "My Sister Gets Married." The anthology also contains "When He Was Free and Young and Used to Wear Silks," one of Austin Clarke's most critically-acclaimed stories. Also included is one of Dionne Brand's finest essays, "Just Rain, Bacolet," excerpts from Dany Laferrière's colourful novel *Dining With The Dictator* and selections from other well-known authors such as Lawrence Hill, Archibald J. Crail and Suzette Mayr. *Eyeing the North Star* showcases an array of intelligent, engaging works that prove African-Canadian writers are finally reaping the benefits of their journey. [*Toronto Star*, 1997]

The Bondwoman's Narrative

by Hannah Crafts;
edited by Henry Louis Gates, Jr.
Warner, 338 pages

In February 2001 Henry Louis Gates's passion for African-American literature led him to a remarkable discovery: a handwritten manuscript of a novel belonging to a fugitive slave in the second half of the 1850s. *The Bondwoman's Narrative* was written by a mulatto named Hannah Crafts. It gives a spirited, and most likely, fictionalized account of her years in slavery and her subsequent escape to the North. Gates believes that Crafts's novel is possibly the first penned by an African-American woman, and certainly the first by a fugitive slave. His thorough, lively introduction documents his largely fruitful efforts to authenticate the work, although the author's true identity—Crafts is likely a literary alias—remains a mystery.

Gates has reproduced the manuscript pretty much as he found it: a polished working draft, with a few changes crossed out and spelling errors left intact. His enthusiasm for the project is contagious. Crafts, a woman of limited education and resources, fashioned a wise and enlightening tale of the peculiar institution from the rarely acknowledged perspective of a slave woman.

From the first paragraph of *The Bondwoman's Narrative*, we are swept into Hannah Crafts's world. She grows up on a vast Virginia plantation called Lindendale. She knows little about her past, is ignorant of the names and whereabouts of her parents and virtually raises herself. A mulatto, who could in fact pass for white, she is spared the harsh work of the fields for the privilege of household duties. In her spare time she sneaks off to meet an old white woman who teaches her to read and instructs her in Christian principles. Over the years, Hannah develops a steady faith that sustains her.

Her narrative reveals a sophisticated synthesis of a number of literary conventions. Her work does share the Victorian writer's unfortunate penchant for cloying piety and remarkable coincidence. Yet it also joins, in original manner, the slave narrative (first-hand accounts of bondage and harrowing escapes) with the ghostly roots of Southern Gothic tradition.

Lindendale embodies the gothic element. Crafts describes the master's home as a large, opulent mansion with numerous unused rooms and echoing corridors. Eerie portraits of generations of De Vincent ancestors line one gallery wall. Next to the house stands an old linden tree with heavy branches that sob in the wind. The wails recall the agonizing cries of brutalized slaves:

> The servants all know the history of that tree. It had not been concealed from them that a wild and weird influence was supposed to belong to it. ... (It) was chosen as the scene where the tortures and punishments were inflicted.

The Bondwoman's Narrative also strikingly foreshadows the intensely nostalgic plantation romance that would explode in popularity at the turn of the twemtieth century. It's curious that this work should appear in the wake of *The Wind Done Gone*, Alice Randall's facetious novel based on Margaret Mitchell's *Gone With The Wind*. Though Hannah Crafts wrote her novel nearly a century before Mitchell's, her heroine might be the slave Prissy made intelligent and kind, and permitted to tell the story.

Like the slaves of plantation romances, who reject freedom to remain with their masters, Hannah, for much of the book, is the most faithful of faithful retainers. When her mistress, Mrs. Vincent, learns that her own black heritage is to be exposed, the two run away together so Hannah can remain her servant.

Both characters belong to that exotic literary type found in nine-teenth-century American fiction, the tragic mulatto. In Hannah's world tragic mulattos are common. Just about every black character in this novel is part white, which serves to underscore the horrific degree to which female slaves were sexually exploited. Slave owners like Cosgrove, who inherits Lindendale, regularly father children with their female chattel, in addition to the offspring they produce with their wives.

Cosgrove's new wife, an English immigrant, is outraged when she learns of her husband's slave "favourites." "I have heard that in this detestable country such things are common," she says. "I heard so before I came here, I know it now." Crafts's novel illuminates the white southerner's quiet, queasy awareness of the unseemly character of the practice of slavery. Even those who own slaves exude scorn for slave traders. More than once, Hannah encounters whites who secretly loathe the institution. One white family she meets after her first failed escape is quietly preparing to free their slaves. The ante-bellum South rang with voices claiming slavery was ordained by God. This novel makes us doubt that many of those people actually believed what they were saying.

Among other things, *The Bondwoman's Narrative* is a black woman's effort to transcend the harsh limitations of slave life, an existence Hannah describes as a malignant emotional strain:

> But those who think that the greatest evils of slavery are connected with physical suffering possess no just or rational ideas of human nature. The soul, the immortal soul must ever long and yearn for a thousand things inseparable to liberty. Then, too, the fear, the apprehension, the dread, and the deep anxiety always attending that condition in a greater or less degree. There can be no certainly, no abiding confidence, in the possession of any good thing.

Hannah's story is just one of the millions of individual stories of the millions of individual people historically lumped together as slaves. Yet, because Hannah Crafts learned to read and write—she was, in fact, a wonderfully literate storyteller—because she was black but looked white and because she had access to both the big house and the slave quarters, she was able to leave us a truer portrait of the pre-Civil War South than any conventional plantation novelist could. With the publication of *The Bondwoman's Narrative*, the wind done gone for good. [*National Post*, 2002]

Crowns: Portraits of Black Women in Church Hats
by Michael Cunningham and Craig Marberry
Doubleday, 212 pages

My mother grew up a Catholic in Kingston, Jamaica. There, in the 1940s, no female was permitted to enter the sanctuary without a hat. This was more or less the norm for churchgoing women around the world, so when my mother arrived in Toronto in the fall of '59, she wasn't surprised to see that Canadian women in her new congregation wore hats as well, though she was baffled by what she perceived as a lack of millinery imagination.

These days, most North American women tend to dress casually. Hats are considered formal attire, too dressy even for church. The dramatic exception to this rule is African-American women. In *Crowns: Portraits of Black Women in Church Hats* photographer Michael Cunningham and author Craig Marberry showcase more than two dozen African-American women in their most dazzling headgear, along-side brief personal essays. Altogether it's a uniquely captivating profile of African-American culture. The pictures are breathtaking, but it's the stories behind the portraits that make this an exhilarating read. Following a foreword by US poet laureate Maya Angelou, the essays illu-minate the significance of church hats in each woman's family history. For Adnee Bradford, a 62-year-old English professor, church hats remind her of how her father loved to see her dressed up. "Sis," he'd say. "Where'd you get that hat?" Boutique owner Audrey Easter recalls the days when hats were a sign of status: "Once you got up on your feet, you bought some hats."

Crowns leaves me pining for the black church I used to attend in west-end Toronto. I was drawn there in search of spiritual guidance. But I was held there by the oratorical flourish, the soul-satiating gospel and a peculiar, paradoxical blend of piety and glamour. Most of the women owned more church clothes than I had in my entire wardrobe. Walking through the door on Sabbath morning one was struck by a kaleidoscope of texture and colour: heavy green silk, airy chiffon, crisp linen criss-crossed with gold. Not all of the women wore headdresses, but many did. From my seat in the balcony, the hats were saucers of nodding colour, wildflowers in a breeze.

There were hats I especially admired. One elegant woman sometimes wore a chocolate-brown suit with a short-waisted, double-breasted jacket and four large black buttons arranged in a square. Her hat was a pillbox, also chocolate brown. It had a dotted black veil that fell down over her eyes and cast mysterious shadows across her cheeks.

Another woman sometimes wore a soft grey Robin Hood cap with a single, silvery plume. It looked as though she had a dove nesting peacefully in her hair. There were a few supple understated cloches. A handful of women favoured a Napoleonic style that floated on the head like a battleship. I was occasionally forced to engage in military-like manoeuvres in order to avoid being trapped behind such a model for an entire service.

Men wore hats too, dimpled fedoras, a dignified fez, dashing black berets, but they doffed their head gear as they arrived. Men whose wives wore hats displayed a particular husbandly pride. And the women themselves exhibited a somewhat regal bearing. Indeed, a slight tilt of the chin was often required to keep an elaborate chapeau in place. The haughty posture discouraged over-familiarity. Hats bestowed upon the wearer an air of aloofness and feminine glamour. Women in hats were ladies, to use an old-fashioned term.

Today, younger black women are opting for complicated hairstyles over hats—lavish updos reminiscent of Audrey Hepburn or The Supremes, architecturally inspired braids. The hairstyles are as attention-grabbing as hats, but require less ladylike attitude to pull off. I sported one such 'do for about a year—a dramatic oval patterned plait that billowed into the shape of a conch. Still, I haven't acquired the confidence to wear a church hat. I remain for the time being a lady-in-waiting. [*National Post*, 1999]

Bud, Not Buddy

by Christopher Paul Curtis

Delacorte, 245 pages

Sometimes when adults write children's books about the value of black history they adopt an earnest tone. They sound as though they are trying to convince themselves, which is a feeling young people pick up on. But in his second novel, *Bud, Not Buddy*, Christopher Paul Curtis conveys the significance of African-American history with a playful touch. Curtis does this so well, in fact, that the American Library Association has awarded him the prestigious John Newberry Medal for the year's best children's book. He has also collected a Coretta Scott King Award for excellence in writing for African-American children. Curtis is the first writer to hold both honours at the same time.

A resident of Windsor, Ontario, Curtis first thrilled readers with his funny, poignant debut novel *The Watsons Go to Birmingham* (1997). The story chronicles a Michigan family's visit to the Deep South during the turbulent civil rights era. Curtis sets *Bud, Not Buddy* in 1936 in Michigan during the harshest years of the Depression.

When we first meet the 10-year-old Bud (not Buddy as he informs everyone he meets), his beloved mother has been dead four years, and he has been residing, off and on, at the orphanage in Flint. One day Bud is sent to live with a well-to-do black family. But when he gets into a fight with the 12-year-old son, his new guardians are predisposed to misjudge him.

"I am not the least bit surprised at your show of ingratitude," barks Bud's foster mother. "Lord knows I have been stung by my own people before. But take a good look at me because I am totally fed up with you and your ilk. I do not have time to put up with the foolishness of those members of our race who do not want to be uplifted." The Amos's attitudes toward poor black people reveal the sharp class distinctions that mark African-American life.

Bud runs away, but decides not to return to the orphanage, which has become crowded with abandoned children. Instead, he sets off in search of a bandleader named Herman E. Calloway, whom he believes to be his father. The evidence is flimsy, but that does not stop Bud from embarking upon the 120-mile journey to Grand Rapids.

Bud's quest to find his father is comical, yet full of intrigue. Along the way he learns about the politics of his country and the condition of his people. He finds himself in the local *Hooverville*. (Named for President Herbert Hoover, *Hoovervilles* were the shantytowns that homeless people erected to provide themselves with shelter.) Both black and white people live in Hooverville, and Curtis subtly suggests that poverty is as much an issue of class as it is of race.

Outside the town of Owosso, Bud is picked up by a kind black man, who is worried to see a black child walking along the road at night. His name is Lefty Lewis and he offers Bud this piece of advice:

> Bud, not Buddy you don't know how lucky you are I came through here, some of these Owosso folks used to have a sign hanging along here that said, and I'm going to clean up the language for you, it said, "To Our Negro Friends Who Are Passing Through, Kindly Don't Let The Sun Set On Your Rear End in Owosso."

Lefty Lewis is a man who likes to make jokes. He tells wildly exaggerated stories, referred to as "lies" or tall tales. Indeed, Curtis shows how the tall tale, an integral aspect of black oral culture, often helped black people handle threatening situations. When Lefty, a union organizer, is pulled over by police, he quickly concocts "a story" that saves himself and Bud.

Bud has also developed a series of survival rules that involve the tall tale. He calls them, "Bud Caldwell's Rules and Things for Having a Funner Life and Making a Better Liar Out of Yourself."

Here is part of Rule #118: *You have to give adults something that they think they can use to hurt you by taking it away. That way they might not take something away that you really do want.*

Bud also understands the instructive value of the old legends. He remembers his mother reading him folk tales at night—tales that taught black people how to survive, and even thrive, in a society that deemed them powerless.

In *Bud, Not Buddy* Curtis incorporates elements of mystery and music. His use of African-American idioms make the novel sing. The story pulses with community spirit. Best of all, Curtis dramatizes African-American history in a way that allows black children to see for themselves the tenacity, wit, wisdom and resourcefulness that defined their ancestors' lives. [*Pride*, 2000]

Slammin' Tar
by Cecil Foster
Random House Canada, 434 pages

Cecil Foster's *Slammin' Tar* is the Barbadian-born author's third and most ambitious novel to date. It unites two storytelling traditions, oral and written, and two peoples, African and European, to narrate the tale of migrant Caribbean labourers on a farm in southern Ontario. As with Foster's last novel, *Sleep On, Beloved*, and his award-winning chronicle of black-Canadian life, *A Place Called Heaven*, *Slammin' Tar* explores the thwarted dreams of West Indians in Canada. Foster approaches this latest effort with the same emotional integrity that marks all his literary endeavours. Unfortunately, a preponderance of complex themes and some bewilderingly slipshod editing sap the work of its potential power.

This is discouraging, because Foster has come up with a truly intriguing premise. He attempts to dramatize the psychological limbo of black Canadian immigrants who feel increasingly less at home in the islands, yet remain unaccepted here. The novel's protagonist, Johnny Franklin, represents a kind of Bajan working-class Everyman. A 42-year-old husband and father of three, Johnny has been with the Canadian migrant labour program for twenty-five years. He is one of a dozen or so men who spend ten months of each year at Edgecliff, a struggling Ontario tobacco farm. Johnny is joined by his best friend, Tommy, who suffers from a lingering cough, and Albert, who hopes his staunch adherence to the program's rules will encourage immigration officials to allow him to settle in Canada.

Then there is Winston, the newest and youngest member of the team, who nearly heads straight back to Barbados after he encounters the brutal winter and the dilapidated cabin the workers call home. Even so, the men stay in the program because their families need the money. Secretly, some dream of "slammin' tar"—of running away from the farm—even if it means life as an illegal immigrant.

Johnny's story is narrated by Anansi, the fantastic spider of African oral folklore, whose stories provide moral lessons and mythical explications of the world. In *Slammin' Tar*, the motif works best when Anansi employs his tales to share wisdom and warnings.

However, Anansi seriously interferes with the character's ability to engage the reader. Rather than allowing us to decipher the men's actions, Foster uses Anansi to communicate the meaning of virtually every facial twitch and shoulder shrug. What's more, the spider's incessant, meandering soliloquies slow the pace unbearably.

Still, Anansi's speeches do make a number of significant historical parallels. He compares the migration of Caribbean labour to Canada with the forced migration of African slaves. He also attempts to draw an analogy between Johnny Franklin and Marcus Garvey, leader of the United Negro Improvement Association, who in the 1920's urged blacks to return to their ancestral home of Africa. The Anansi narrative also compares the farm labourers' precarious financial situation with the near-bankruptcy of their employer, George Stewart, owner of Edgecliff Farm. Foster places a heavy thematic load on the back of one tiny spider.

By all rights, Edgecliff should emerge from the novel as forcefully as any character. After all, the fortunes of practically every figure in the story depend on the farm's survival or demise. But Foster allows so little time with the labourers in the field that we end up with hardly any idea of their physical relationship to this foreign landscape.

At several points in the novel I wondered, "Where was Foster's editor?" What excuse could there be for allowing the word "courteous" to crop up four times in two paragraphs. How to explain the appearance of countless clichés: characters who "bite the dust," exhibit "zest for life," and "march to their own drum."

A number of people have suggested to me that white editors sometimes feel hesitant about criticizing the work of black authors. They fear their comments may be perceived as racist. But that seems a bit of a cop-out. White people fear saying something racist largely because they are unfamiliar with black culture. An editor who is too uncomfortable with an author to admit the need to know more about the writer's literary tradition is probably not the right editor for that job.

Besides, anyone who really wants to find out about a particular tradition could simply read up on it. Still, the dilemma is a useful illustration of why Canada's book (add newspaper and publishing) industry needs to build an ethnically diverse body of editors. While the vast majority of Caribbean authors writing in Canada (Austin Clarke, Rachel Manley, Olive Senior, Dany Laferrière, for example) structure their narratives in the British tradition, more and more often a publisher will need to find editors with specific cultural knowledge.

I cannot say with any confidence that editorial timidity hurt Foster's novel. I can say however, that what could have been an original, enduring work will likely be remembered as a rather spectacular failure. How disappointing. [*Globe and Mail*, 1998]

Any Known Blood
by Lawrence Hill
Harper Collins, 512 pages

L awrence Hill's second novel, *Any Known Blood*—his first was the well-received *Some Great Thing*—is an expansive tale about five generations of a black Canadian family. It might also be a good idea to say upfront what this book is not. It is not a dramatized jeremiad of wrongs inflicted upon the African peoples. And it is not the embodiment of their diasporic journey. Nor is this novel the story of a race. Rather, *Any Known Blood* follows one man's frequently hilarious, often romantic, sometimes poignant trek through family history along the road to self-discovery.

Langston Cane V lives in Toronto where he works as a speechwriter for a parsimonious provincial government that bears a suspicious resemblance to Ontario's ruling Tories. But he gets fired after writing a speech that leaks the contents of a confidential document. Langston suggests that the error was inadvertent, but he is a narrator that we cannot always trust. For one thing, although he hails from Oakville, Ontario, and he is of mixed race parentage (black and white) Langston likes to pretend he belongs to any number of nationalities. He has claimed to be Moroccan and Peruvian and Jamaican and Sikh. He landed his government job by concocting an Algerian heritage.

Langston's antics mask a genuine insecurity about identity. He is uncertain about his place in a long line of accomplished black men, all named Langston Cane. He envies his younger brother Sean, whose thriving law practice and indisputably brown skin better fit the family mold. With a recently failed marriage and a collapsed career behind him, 38-year-old Langston feels like a loser—and his domineering father, the pompous Dr. Langston Cane IV, entirely agrees. Langston decides to prove them both wrong by heading to Baltimore, where he plans to write a novel about his family's history. The stories he uncovers link up to form *Any Known Blood*.

Langston hopes his encounter with the past will provide him with a sense of identity, a means of inhabiting the Canes's lofty tradition, while remaining his own man. By writing *Any Known Blood*, Hill reveals his own similar objective, only he aims to situate himself within a literary tradition. He names his protagonist 'Langston' after the venerable African-American poet Langston Hughes (with whom he shares the initials LH) and he gives his main characters the surname Cane, the title of a groundbreaking early twentieth-century novel by African-American Jean Toomer.

At the same time, Hill shapes conventional black history into his own idiosyncratic, distinctly Canadian form. He anchors his novel in Oakville which, between the mid-nineteenth century and early twentieth centuries, possessed a sizable black community. From the time the first Langston Cane arrived in Oakville as a fugitive slave in the 1850s, all the Canes—even those who eventually return to Baltimore—consider Canada their home.

Hill's use of a witty, self-deprecating first person narrator alters the sober tone generally reserved for African-American history. Indeed, some readers may find it unsettling to read humorous anecdotes in the same novel as stories of slavery and racial hardship. But Hill's sparkling, witty dialogue is one of the chief reasons this five hundred plus page novel is so pleasurable a read. In Langston Cane, Hill creates a true master of the glib rejoinder. In fact, the more Canes there are in a given scene, the more the repartee soars.

The novel's ironic tone fosters a psychological distance that comes in handy when Hill wants to turn racist incidents into absurd, farcical affairs. When members of the Ku Klux Klan burn a cross at Langston III's Oakville home, an outraged black woman attacks. She punches one Klansman in the nose, chases another home and then rips the white sheet off a third. Occasionally, though, Hill's efforts to keep things light result in a loss of socio-historical context, as in the passages chronicling the courtship of Rose and Langston III, which are set around the First World War.

Langston unearths significant information about his ancestors from boxes in the basement of his Aunt Millicent's Baltimore home. He learns that he is not so different from the other Cane men after all. He shares some of his grandfather's strengths (they both save the life of a young boy), and some of his weaknesses as well—he was not the only Cane to commit adultery.

Hill devotes a great deal of space to the Cane marriages, particularly the rocky, romantic union of Langston III and his wife Rose, which he bases upon the relationship of his own paternal grandparents. His deliciously erotic scenes celebrate the passion and playfulness of emotionally intimate bonds. The Cane men not only love their women, they actually like them too.

This novel fairly brims over with joy and affection, although considering the family feuds, dissolved marriages, major wars and racial injustices, it's hard to say why. I suppose the answer lies in the humanity of Hill's characters, the fullness of the lives he has conceived. He has written a novel of which his ancestors—literary and otherwise—would be proud. [*Globe and Mail*, 1997]

Brown Girl in the Ring
by Nalo Hopkinson
Warner, 256 pages

With *Brown Girl in the Ring* Nalo Hopkinson takes readers on a sci-fi excursion into a phantasmagoric Toronto of the not-too-distant future. Warner Aspect published Hopkinson's debut effort after she won first place in the Warner Books First Novel Contest in September, 1997. Hopkinson, who came from Jamaica to Canada at the age of 16, was up against nearly one thousand candidates from all over the world.

Her story takes place in a city that has been ravaged by riots and abandoned by its wealthier inhabitants. Companies and banks have departed, as have the police and medical services. The city stinks of out-houses (the sanitation workers are gone too), and reels from a battery of constant crime. A ganglord named Rudy Sheldon has replaced local government. He rules through a posse of stupid, violent men.

Even though we are some years into the millenium (Hopkinson doesn't specify), Toronto remains unsettlingly familiar. Rudy runs his evil operation from inside the CN Tower, and Ti-Jeanne, the novel's young female heroine, resides with her grandmother in the façade of a house on the Riverdale Farm. Ti-Jeanne's grandmother, Gros-Jeanne, raises goats and chickens. She also grows plants and herbs for her healing practice. A bushdoctor in the Afro-Carib tradition, Gros-Jeanne boasts the gift of visionary powers.

Ti-Jeanne has visions as well. But she rejects her grandmother's attempts to pass on her special inheritance. Indeed, Ti-Jeanne wants nothing to do with the past or family traditions. Rather, she would happily reunite with Tony, the father of her baby, and move as a family to the suburbs.

Hopkinson's novel could be described as social-science fiction. But it smoothly encompasses a variety of genres. The premise, for example, is reminiscent of Jonathan Swift's satirical essays: Ontario's premier is in need of a heart transplant and the hospital nefariously asks Rudy to find them a fresh urban victim. Rudy in turn orders Ti-Jeanne's Tony to murder a healthy person and extract the heart. Instead, the terrified Tony asks Gros-Jeanne to help him escape the city. *Brown Girl in the Ring* evolves into a spine-chilling horror story that draws Rudy's dark powers into conflict with Afro-Caribbean spirituality.

Perhaps more than other genres, sci-fi carries the burden of expounding a message. But Hopkinson's marvellous tonal control enables her to elude this pitfall. Though the words "Toronto" and "riots" recall the melee over Rodney King, and though "posse" is a favourite buzzword for those who like to link Jamaicans with crime, and though a significant portion of the remaining Toronto inhabitants possess Caribbean heritage, race remains a subtle backdrop to the action of the novel.

What one comes away with is the suffering city's tenacious spirit of community. Without money, people barter for goods. They take over public parks and build farms. Street children protect one another and ailing individuals turn to midwives and healers like Gros-Jeanne. In the midst of evil and destruction, suggests Hopkinson, one discovers alcoves of kindness. [*Quill & Quire*, 1998]

Rush Home Road

by Lori Lansens

Knopf Canada, 547 pages

Lori Lansens' novel *Rush Home Road*, which earned a six-figure American advance and which publishers are hyping as a new Canadian classic, consists of two tenuously wedded stories. The first is a polished, modest tale set in a shabby trailer park outside Chatham, Ontario. It is here, in 1980, that a black woman named Addy Shadd takes in Sharla, an abandoned mixed-race girl. Addy quickly comes to love Sharla as her own, but the aging woman wonders who will care for the child when she is gone.

Sharla, the daughter of a neglectful white mother and an unknown black father, is the novel's inspired creation. Lansens proves her potential by the way she dreams herself into the heart of this sweetly jaded youngster. "Sharla liked the looks of Addy Shadd and thought how no one had ever called her honey before. She felt like she'd like to pat down Addy Shadd's sparkly white hair. She felt like she'd like to kiss Addy Shadd's pucker-bum mouth and to sit in her skinny lap and bury her nose in the folds of her neck."

Addy's wise, mature voice is also well-tuned, and her deepening relationship with the awkward Sharla—a modern take on the traditional mammy/child bond—is finely expressed.

The other story in this two-tiered novel is managed with less success. It opens in the black town of Rusholme, also near Chatham, in the early decades of the twentieth century, when disgrace, a rape and a pregnancy—plus a tragedy, the deaths of three men—drive Addy from her community.

Lansens bases Rusholme on an actual southwestern Ontario town established in the nineteenth century as a haven for escaped American slaves. The surname Shadd belongs to one of the region's most prominent families. But Addy is not related to this caring, prestigious bunch. After her callous parents turn her out, the heavily pregnant girl undertakes a frightening journey to Detroit, where she remains for some time before settling in Chatham. The uncomplaining woman endures a life streaked with loss. Through it all she yearns to return to her beloved Rusholme.

Lansens presents us with a time and place as steeped in history as the American South; rich material indeed. But her unsophisticated grasp of black experience, and her unseasoned literary skills, prevent her from making much out of it. Part of Lansens' problem is our correct Canadian culture, which insists there is no such thing as a black Canadian experience distinct from a white Canadian experience. It's difficult for Canadian writers of any race to dramatize a phenomenon they are not convinced exists.

Lansens' novel does nothing to alleviate this cloud of racial confusion. Instead, she unwittingly casts her own mixed feelings in language. One example is Addy and Sharla's trailer park, which has become segregated over time. Addy does not take the racial division to heart:

> The trailer park was never meant to be separated, but it worked out that a few coloured folks bought up some of the cheaper lots and trailers on the unpaved land in the sixties. More came and more, and even those who could afford to buy on the paved lands came to the mud land instead. It was just natural to want to be near your people.

Addy acts as though she believes that segregation is a choice black people happily make. In so doing, she denies the brutal slave history and the harsh Canadian attitudes that led to the establishment of her black hometown, the place she refers to repeatedly as a source of racial pride.

But then, the story's very premise would appear to dismiss the town's tortured past. It seems implausible that this particular community would turn Addy over to a daunting white world simply because she is unwed and pregnant. After all, this is a town recently founded as a home for slaves, many of whom could never have known the identity of their fathers. Lansens' unwillingness to contemplate how slave history might impact on the actions and sentiments of her black characters severely compromises the integrity of her story.

Lansens is an accomplished screenwriter, but *Rush Home Road* is her first novel, and it shows. Rusholme comprises the heart of this story and yet the reader never empathizes with her feelings for the town. Lansens does not give us opportunity to properly acquaint ourselves with the area and, as a result, Addy's memories never become our own.

There are lesser dilemmas of craft; technical quandaries that reveal Lansens as an uncertain practitioner. Significantly, these shortcomings are overwhelmingly restricted to the historical passages and rarely arise in chapters concerning Sharla and the aging Addy. The novel may have worked better had all the material been smoothly rolled into this one story, instead of chopped up into two. Nevertheless, *Rush Home Road* has a sweetness and charm about it. As well, Addy Shadd is a brave and amiable character. Yet she is something of a stick figure. Unlike major African-American heroines, she remains disconnected from a particular history and people and place, which is precisely the way we Canadians prefer to perceive black people. [*Toronto Star*, 2002]

The Book of Ifs and Buts
by Rabindranath Maharaj
Vintage, 314 pages

The immigrant experience is a central trope in Canadian literature. Rabindranath Maharaj's new collection of stories, *The Book of Ifs and Buts*, supplies a fresh, imaginative and moving interpretation of the theme. Maharaj, a Trinidadian of Indian descent, arrived in Canada in 1993. His first collection, *The Interloper* (1995), was nominated for a Commonwealth Writer's Prize and his novel *Homer in Flight* (1998) was shortlisted for the Chapters/Books In Canada First Novel Award. *The Book of Ifs and Buts* follows in a similar vein.

In the collection, men and women abandon Eastern Europe or the Caribbean to embark on new lives in North America. Maharaj charts their high hopes and slim accomplishments and observes their protracted suspension between two worlds. Slyly disregarding the socially realistic approach, he subtly introduces mystical, folkloric elements into seemingly conventional narratives. Most important, these stories use the immigrant experience to examine a question that obsesses both literature and the human heart: How does the past relate to the present?

The book opens with "The Journey of Angels," a novella-length story featuring Saren, an Armenian gardener living in Brooklyn. Unprepossessing and kind, Saren is happy enough with his new position. But urban America's crude isolation unsettles him deeply. Ultimately, Saren relies on elements of his past—the books of a former employer—to concoct a new identity. The alias eases him through a period of adjustment.

Through most of the book, characters treat emigration as a watershed event. But Saren struggles to accept his move to America as a single episode in a life-long odyssey. He does not see his Armenian past as severed from his American present, but as part of a continuum.

Many of Maharaj's characters revere books as repositories of knowledge and tools for advancement in the New World. The most successful also retain the mystical faith of their ancestors. "Swami" Pankaj is a gifted Trinidadian farmer living in Canada who fantasizes about eventually settling in the Himalayas. In the meantime, he embarrasses his upwardly mobile community by wearing traditional dress and spouting spiritual truths. Still, it is determination sustained by the power of faith that enables Pankaj to achieve his dream.

Virtually every central character in this book could be described as an outsider, even a misfit. Maharaj sometimes burdens his characters with physical deformities as a measure of their otherness. In "The Journey of Angels," Saren's chronic back ailment twists into deformity, and the teacher in the "House on Lengua Street" claims he is so ugly that people keep their distance. These grotesque traits symbolize the immigrant's alienation from the wider population. They also represent our essential isolation as individual human beings, the loneliness we strive to conquer through community and/or love.

There are nine tales altogether, many of which, like folk tales, draw attention to themselves as stories. Maharaj, for all his obvious love of books, is always reminding the reader to keep things in perspective. Stories may hold meaning, he seems to say, but they are still just stories. "The Journey of Angels," an alluring blend of nonchalance and sincere sentiment, displays the same sophisticated style that characterizes the work of Alice Munro and Richard Ford. It will undoubtedly earn the highest praise. On the other hand, one or two of the narratives slip into cliché. But all of them have their charms which rely to varying degrees on humour and voice. Maharaj has a marvellous, effortless way with dialect: "Haul you mangy little ass from here," the West Indian butcher snarls in "Laugh Now."

The last story, "The House in Lengua Street" is my favourite. The narrator is a prodigal son who returns to Trinidad after a thirty-three-year absence. He is estranged from his father and siblings, and from his wife, who remains in Canada. Arriving unannounced, he finds his father on his deathbed. The house, a decaying shadow, haunts him with vivid memories. He is nearly senseless with loss and regret, but all he can do is work through it.

As a rule, many Canadian writers depict the struggle as a conflict between the emigrant and his new surroundings, and this depiction is accurate and fair. But Maharaj is superb at portraying the emigrant's inner struggle, the conflict between past and present that we all experience whether we emigrate or not. He articulates the psychological blocks that hinder a person from moving forward, or back. Then he turns such unlikely material into the stuff of legend. [*National Post*, 2003]

Putting Down Roots: Montreal's Immigrant Writers

By Elaine Kalman Naves
Véhicule Press, 178 pages

On this cool spring evening, about one hundred people have gathered at Chapters on rue Ste-Catherine in Montreal for a reading featuring the authors from *Putting Down Roots: Montreal's Ethnic Writers*. People whisper restlessly, in English and in French, anxious for the event to begin. It is not often that the anglo/francophone debate leaves space enough for other voices, and there is a certain excitement in the air. The controversial Italian-born playwright Marco Micone is first. He prefaces a reading from his play *Gens du silence* with separatist remarks guaranteed to irritate his peers. The barrel-chested Hungarian poet György Vitéz looks slightly irked. Vitez will soon rise to recite a tender paean to the idea of home. Micone also seems to have perturbed Rana Bose, a tall slender South Asian playwright. But Bose will set aside his annoyance to delight us with a passage about a man of strenuously mixed heritage.

Later the statuesque Haitian poet Marie-Celie Agnan, striking in turban and shawl, will sweep to the podium to deliver a dramatic oration. And finally, John Asfour, the blind Lebanese poet, is guided to the dais to celebrate his father's arrival in 1960s Montreal. For an hour or so we are transfixed by their stories—the tales of those who weave new lives from past identites and present circumstance. And little by little grows the idea that another Quiet Revolution is taking place.

What we feel here is something of what French officials must have felt at the recent Salon du livre in Paris, when they laid eyes on Quebec's ethnically diverse contingent. The delegation included Ying Chen, a native of Shanghai and author of the impressive novel *L'Ingratitude*, Japanese-born Ook Chung and the Iraqi writer Naïm Kattan, as well as the more familiar faces of Neil Bissoondath, Emile Ollivier and Dany Laferrière. Though ethnic writers accounted for only a portion of the total number of visiting artists, numerous French articles appeared proclaiming a new multicultural Quebec literature.

Some, including Dany Laferrière, saw the French media's astonishment as naive or even mendacious. How could France imagine a Quebec untouched by the immigration waves of recent years? The answer surely lies with the province's policy of distinct identity, which encourages notions of a French monoculture.

Elaine Kalman Naves, a popular book columnist for the Montreal *Gazette*, has been writing about the city's diverse literary community for several years. Her columns were the basis for her first book on the topic, entitled *The Writers of Montreal* (1993).

Her second collection, *Putting Down Roots*, features Quebec writers who feel their ethnicity leaves them out of the French-English matrix. The best known is Chava Rosenfarb, whose award winning epic *Tree of Life* (1972) portrays Poland's Lodz ghetto, and there is Ramon Guardia whose *El bengalii* (1985) eerily prefigured the Oka crisis. Naves depicts a city that is home to a club that promotes Hungarian classics and to a bookstore that offers the largest selection of Arabic titles on the continent. She acknowledges an arts scene so diverse, so vital and yet so generally unrecognized that it was left to Mordecai Richler to institute an award. Dubbed the Prix Parizeau, the prize honours the achievements of Quebecois writers Richler facetiously dubbed *impure laine*.

In *Putting Down Roots* Naves' keeps her discussion of Montreal's literary multiculturalism apolitical. This Hungarian-born daughter of Holocaust survivors "is interested in biographical terms, not political terms." Yet even she would agree that it is impossible to avoid politics when you are an immigrant writer in Montreal. Although you are labelled an outsider, you are often forced to take a position. The language you choose to write in—English or French—has profound implications. So does the decision whether or not to write about your particular cultural experience. If you do wind up writing about your particular cultural experience, your work is likely to be perceived as a threat to Quebec's distinct society.

The Haitian writers who fled the Duvalier regime posed little threat to nationalist ideals when they arrived in Montreal in the mid-1960s. On the contrary, both francophone and Catholic, Haitian artists became early allies. For centuries, Haiti and Montreal were considered the two main centres of French culture outside of Europe. As people of African descent, Haitians identified with the Quebecois sense of oppression. During the Quiet Revolution, they often met with their Montreal counterparts. In cafés along rue Metcalfe they shared ideas about Negritude, the African nationalist movement, with the likes of Claude Gauvreau, Gaston Miron and Michel Beaulieu.

Emile Ollivier remembers those days. Among the most esteemed of Haitian Canadian writers, Ollivier has earned numerous awards for novels such as *Passages* (1991) and *Mère Solitude* (1983). He describes to Naves the heady blend of literature and politics that marked the times: "This was the time when Pierre Vallieres brought out his *White Niggers of America*," he says. "We felt there was a kind of coalescence going on, a mayonnaise that had taken."

Unlike the francophone Haitian, Italian-Canadian writers have been compelled to choose a language. Although the poets Mary Melfi and Mary di Michele work in English, and others, such as Marco Micone and Mario Campo, opt for French, all mull over the problem of abandoning their native tongue.

Born in the Molise region of Italy in 1945, Micone arrived in Canada in 1958. He enrolled first in English schools, but switched to French as soon as he grasped the politics. Unlike the overwhelming majority of this fellow Italians, Micone feels great empathy for the separatist cause.

"I came from a region in Italy that was oppressed," he says. "I learned Italian as a second language. I had a teacher who came into the class each day with a list of Italian words for us to learn. Even though my community demanded that the schoolchildren be taught the regional dialect, it remained a dream never realized.

"When I came to Quebec I found that the French people here had the same problem—but I am Quebeois with a difference. I want the Quebecois to deal with all the complexities of my identity, including the fact that I am nostalgic for the place where I was born."

Thirty years after arriving in Montreal from shattered Lebanon, John Asfour is still wondering about how, even in peaceful environments, people find issues to fight about. When Asfour was a child, out playing with his friends, an innocent-looking contraption blew up in his face. Over the next few years, Asfour slowly went blind.

The author, who has written three books of poetry and edited one collection, *When the Words Burn: An Anthology of Modern Arabic Poetry, 1945-1987* (1992), says he does not wish to trivialize the tensions between the French and the English. "I understand that language is very important," he says, "especially when French has excluded you from the...bounty of the country." Still, he knows first-hand what can happen when societal tensions are not resolved. For Asfour, language is finally less a tool for politics, than a means of communication. The poems in *Fields of My Blood* (1997) convey the immigrant's feelings about coming to a new land. His poem "Flight," which imagines arriving at Dorval airport in 1968, describes the feelings of every hopeful immigrant to Quebec:

My sons are confused by the absence
of a brass band tailed by dancing girls
or envy from Pierre Trudeau
requesting our presence
at a small soiree.
They tack between signs bearing languages
that I will never read.

We are invited only
to show a visa—daredevils who have
in under twelve hours, browsed in three continents, reshaped a
village,
strewn the husks
off our ambitions through the clouds.

Asfour's poem, like Naves's *Putting Down Roots*, conveys the particu-
larities of the immigrant experience in Montreal, as well as the essence
of the experience for millions of others everywhere. [*National Post*, 2000]

Kipligat's Chance
By David Odhiambo
Penguin, 274 pages

Did you ever hear the African folk tale about how wisdom was spread? Long, long ago an old man named Kwaku Ananse had all the wisdom in the world. But he was a selfish man and did not want to share his good fortune with anyone. Kwaku decided he would collect his wisdom into a large pot and hide it at the top of a tall tree. One dark night he tied the pot of wisdom to his back. He found a tall tall tree and tried to climb it. But the pot was large and awkward and Kwaku made slow progress.

Suddenly laughter rang out behind him. Kwaku turned around and saw his son Ntikuma. The boy was bent in two, laughing at the spectacle his father made climbing with a pot on his back. Kwaku hated to be laughed at. He untied the big pot and tossed it at his son. Little pieces of wisdom floated everywhere. And that's how wisdom was spread.

It looks like some of that wisdom found its way into *Kipligat's Chance*, the second novel by Vancouver's David Odhiambo. It's a coming-of-age story about a 16-year-old Kenyan emigrant and the trials he faces while struggling to become a track star. The novel combines the author's affection for proverbs, so prevalent in his native Kenya, with an appreciation for English literature, especially Shakespeare. Indeed, the novel reads very much like an expanded proverb or modern day fable. It is pithy, witty, wise and unpretentious.

The story is set in a seedy section of Vancouver in the late 1970s when John "Leeds" Kipligat and his best friend Kulvinder win spots on a select track team. The pair hopes for college scholarships. But John's road is littered with obstacles, including his father's irascible nature, his mother's illness, his increasingly combative relationship with Kulvinder and the loss of true love. John eventually learns that "the race is not always to the swiftest, but to the one who can keep on moving."

In African culture, elders hold a special place as the keepers of traditional knowledge. It is said that when an old man dies, it's as if an entire library has burnt to the ground. In *Kipligat's Chance*, John's coach Sam, a flabby smoker, makes an unlikely elder. But it is the annoying perpetual advice of this former Olympian that most encourages the young runner: "Remember," quotes Sam. "To be better lots, you have to be lots better."

Odhiambo gets the dub inspired voice of his teenage hero just right. The reader not only identifies with John, but the jazzy, improvisational, superbly executed prose invites us to read with the abandon of a child. John remembers what it was like to run in Kenya, where he felt like "a kite pulled into the blue sky." So do we.

Despite his warm and lively nature, John is in serious trouble. He is traumatized by the loss of his older brother Koech, a track star and political activist, who is missing somewhere in Kenya. Most effective are italicized scenes—John's memories of Koech and life in Kenya—that rise up in the narrative like dusty dreams.

John is also distressed by racism, which often leaves him feeling ambushed. All this he endures in addition to natural bouts of adolescent self-loathing. Whenever the pressures mount, John locks himself in the bathroom where he slices his arms with a razor.

John sees track as the only way out. In Kenya, where his father had been a high government official, the Kipligats lived in a lovely home. In Vancouver they occupy the lower apartment in a run-down flat on a street frequented by prostitutes. John's mother earns money caring for an invalid child. Her teaching certificate is worthless in Canada. His father seems to have given up on the idea of finding work.

The Kipligats' experience is common to many who would describe themselves as new Canadians. Kulvinder is still reeling from the death of his father in Kenya. A member of Kenya's wealthy merchant class, Kulvinder cannot come to terms with his loss of status in Canada. He drinks and acts out violently against women.

John falls in love with Svetlana, a Polish immigrant. Her father, like John's, had been a government official before settling in Canada. John thinks the two families have much in common. But when he shows up at Svetlana's house unannounced, her father goes after him with a bat. He is outraged that his daughter is dating a black man. The scene has a comic zaniness about it, but Odhiambo makes his point: all immigrants to Canada are not considered equal.

Odhiambo's skill at defining and articulating the black Canadian experience sets him apart from many black Canadian writers. Part of his success comes from the clever blend of subtlety, irony, anger and frustration with which he addresses racism.

Odhiambo's observations about race and class play out within the dynamics of John's four-member track team. Kulvinder falls in love with his elegant teammate Erica, who is black, because she represents to him the upper class. Yet, he does not take her home to meet his Indian mother.

John, on the other hand, cannot abide Erica's snooty ways. He is attracted, instead, to Vivian, whose family history fits the stereotype of

African-American ghetto life. Here again, Odhiambo proves original; it is rare for a black writer to create a male character that exhibits empathy and affection for women of the black underclass.

The novel spans the course of the school year. At first John's emotional woes weaken his commitment to running. After a while, these same difficulties become his motivation. He realizes all obstacles must be overcome if one intends to succeed. Which recalls the proverb made famous by Dr. Martin Luther King:

If you can't fly, run.
If you can't run, walk.
If you can't walk, crawl.
But whatever you do, keep moving.

[*Toronto Star*, 2003]

Frontiers: Essays and Writings on Racism and Culture

M. Nourbese Philip
Mercury, 288 pages

Few incidents so raised the collective ire of African-Canadians as the Royal Ontario Museum's exhibit "Into the Heart of Africa." Nearly three years later, accusations of racism and colonial mentality still reverberate. Author Marlene Nourbese Philip placed herself in the centre of that controversy with a series of outspoken essays. In them she confronted the museum's ethnocentricity and challenged the cultural establishment to recognize and address the problem.

Philip includes her writings on the ROM and a number of other subjects in her recently published collection *Frontiers: Essays and Writings on Racism and Culture. Frontiers* reveals how racism keeps Canadian culture the reserve of white artists and audiences, effectively silencing "other" voices.

Philip is intimately acquainted with the category of "other." A black Canadian writer of Caribbean heritage, she describes herself as perpetually in exile. By her mid-teens she had lived on three islands: Tobago, Trinidad and Jamaica. Canada has been her home now for some twenty-five years. With two novels and three books of poetry to her name, Philip has been awarded the Casa de las Americas prize and she is a Guggenheim Fellow. She remains, nonetheless, an outsider to the Canadian literary scene.

Philip's profile rose dramatically in 1989, after an altercation with journalist June Callwood outside a gathering of the PEN Congress. She had been distributing leaflets protesting the absence of writers of colour from the Canadian delegation. Since then she's maintained her unpopular habit of disturbing Canadian icons. In *Frontiers*, Philip asserts that multicultural divisions in arts councils and other funding bodies often work against the very artists they are trying to help. In "Multicultural Whitewash" Philip writes that minority "artists who are not merely concerned with heritage or preservation for its own sake, ought in funding matters, to be assessed as objectively as other artists."

She charges that the controversy over the censorship of white authors obscures the essential issues: the conflict should not focus on white artists and their use of "other" voices, but on the number of whites receiving funding to tell "minority" stories while minority artists go without.

Frontiers suffers somewhat from the time lapse between the original publication of the articles (most of them appeared in the magazine *Fuse* between 1986 and 1991) and the book's release. Another problem lies in the inevitable redundancy of a single author tackling similar subjects. Still, thoughtful analysis, humour and a vigilant lexicon overshadow these flaws.

Philip touches on a wide range of topics besides the arts: feminism, native rights and war, to name a few. Her essays draw uncommon parallels. In one instance she calls former Manitoba MLA Elijah Harper the Rosa Parks of the Meech Lake Accord. (Parks being the black woman who precipitated the '60s civil rights crisis by refusing to move to the back of the bus.)

The points of reference in this collection are overwhelmingly Canadian. Even so, Philip, like other minority writers, must ask herself: who's listening? *Frontiers* might end up merely preaching to the converted or it could help drag us out of the multicultural morass. [*Toronto Star*, 1992]

No Crystal Stair
by Mairuth Sarsfield
Moulin, 247 pages

Mairuth Sarsfield approaches her first novel, *No Crystal Stair*, with the same energetic ambition she has used to tackle her career. Born in Quebec in 1930, Sarsfield worked as an information officer for External Affairs before moving, in the early '80s, to New York, to become deputy director of the UN's environment program.

In *No Crystal Stair*, however, the author's customary zealousness taxes her nascent abilities as she attempts to weave a diverse array of themes and plots into a complex historical setting. The story offers a fictionalized account of Little Burgundy, the black community in Montreal, where Sarsfield grew up. Set during the economically restrained years of the Second World War, *No Crystal Stair* follows the travails of Marian Willow, a widow who struggles to instill her two daughters with pride in their African heritage. Like most black Canadian women of the era, Marian works as a domestic; in the mornings she keeps house for a separatist female lawyer and in the afternoons she hastens over to the local YMCA where she cleans rooms alongside a number of close friends. Marian's main dilemma concerns whether or not she should marry Edmond Thompson, a handsome railway porter. Edmond's staid, sober nature and the fact he keeps a glamorous mistress, causes Marian to repeatedly defer. Edmond and his nephew Otis, also a porter, work to organize a union that would improve conditions for black men on the Canadian railway.

Sarsfield means for the triangle of Marian, Edmond and Torrie, Edward's lover, to comprise the novel's most compelling conflict. But she compromises the women's authenticity by basing them on anachronistic stereotypes. Despite Marian's status as widow, Sarsfield casts her as the virginal ingenue, who with her fair-skinned desirability rather insidiously summons images of the nineteenth-century mulatto figure. Torrie, on the other hand, plays the role of carnal, worldly woman whose sexual sophistication makes her morally suspect.

Although Sarsfield overextends herself by creating too many extraneous storylines, her secondary characters better manifest her imaginative gifts, particularly the Willow's neighbours, the former Russian consort Dame Orlova Braithwaite and her mixed-race teenage daughter Marushka.

Disappointingly, Sarsfield fails to develop the novel's deeper metaphorical possibilities. *No Crystal Stair*, the title of a Langston Hughes poem, signifies the racial impediments that hinder a black person's journey through life. Yet Sarsfield hardly begins to explore the motif's rich potential. She does attempt to build the railway, which barrels through the community, into a symbol of oppression, but the metaphor evolves fitfully and without much grace.

Sarsfield aims to tell an enduring story about black Canadians in which the dilemma of racism exists, but does not entirely dominate, as it tends to do in "serious" black literature. The problem is that it is difficult to dramatize the unpleasantness of racism with the same voice that one might use to narrate *Little Women*. Irony is a quality that seems to elude Sarsfield altogether, and for a writer hoping to communicate the complexity of the black experience, such artlessness amounts to a fatal flaw. [*Toronto Star*, 1997]

In Silence the Strands Unravel
by Sybil Seaforth
Capricornus, 177 pages

Silence. Rhymes with violence. Although the assonance had never before occurred to me until I read Jamaican Sybil Seaforth's latest novel *In Silence the Strands Unravel*. The strands Seaforth refers to are the ties of matrimony. Her story closely examines one woman's response to the steady deterioration of her marriage.

Jessica Bright has been married to her husband Lionel for thirty years. They have raised three children together in the West Indian city of La Porta. But Lionel has started shutting Jessica out of his life and by the time the novel begins the two are barely speaking.

Talk about your "passive-aggressives." Lionel abruptly cuts off every conversation Jessica begins, even when only the most simple response is required. Jessica is confused and deeply wounded by her husband's behaviour. To the reader, though, Lionel appears calculated and even diabolical. He uses silence as an axe to hack away at his wife's self-esteem. He might admit outright that he is in love with someone else, but he is too cowardly to utter the words that would liberate him with dignity from his status.

Although one doubts that such a confession would alleviate Jessica's sense of injustice at being tossed aside. For she is trapped in a miasma of memories, of the history she and Lionel have shared, and of hopes cruelly dashed, all of which obscures her vision. And yet their early years together gave every indication of Lionel's capacity for unkindness. True, he was a good provider, but he was generally insensitive and maintained little interest in her goals. Still, should Jessica be faulted for trying to make the best of an imperfect situation?

In one of a number of finely etched images, Seaforth draws a parallel between Jessica and a bright darting bird: "...sunlight was tracing patterns on my window pane when I woke to the strident chirping of birds. They sounded so delightfully happy! 'Are birds ever unhappy,' I wondered, 'except when they crash into solid objects?'"

The novel is both the story of one failed marriage, and the tale of a culture of failed marriages. All of Jessica's good friends have suffered through similar marital discord. Many of them are divorced. If Lionel's silence carries Jessica to the brink of madness, the words of her sympathetic women friends keep her sane; just as writing in her diary, in effect talking to herself, convinces Jessica that she still exists.

The novel does sometimes come across as one long conversation between Jessica and her friends as there is little in the way of plot development. Dialogue constitutes the main action, so it is a shame when misplaced commas or quotation marks make the conversation difficult to follow. At the same time the discussions between Jessica, Dora and Norma are truly absorbing; they comprise a thinly disguised debate about the motivations of West Indian men, one that would not be out of place in a psychology or sociology text. The women speculate about the fact that each of their emotionally stunted husbands grew up without a father in the home. And they wonder at the need for West Indian men to continually affirm themselves through sexual conquest.

It is all very interesting, although it is disturbing to watch Jessica attempt to somehow validate Lionel's behaviour. As a result she comes close to appearing pathetic, which she is not. She is humourous and supportive of her friends, she is a wonderful and beloved mother. She also contributes enthusiastically to a community that holds her in high regard.

In addition, Jessica is never too despondent to appreciate her natural surroundings. She is touched, always, by the sight of green shoots pressing up through brown soil and she is comforted by the dependable presence of the mountains. Says Jessica, "There is a timelessness about mountains and mighty trees and the ocean that leave me in awe."

Jessica's major weakness is that she finds it difficult to let go of the promises of the past. (Don't we all). Along with her girlfriends, she recalls the sentimental old songs that lulled her into a fascination with romance. She faults society for providing young women with a false set of values and expectations.

In Silence the Strands Unravel left me feeling that happy marriages are more the exception than the rule. And indeed, Seaforth's Jessica Bright cannot decide whether she should view her broken relationship as a personal failure, or the inevitable consequence of a tired institution. She wonders if she has spent more than half of her life aspiring to a myth. [*Pride*, 2000]

Deemed Unsuitable
by R. Bruce Shepard
Umbrella Press, 150 pages

Many Canadians feel pride about their country's role in the operation of the Underground Railroad. But Saskatchewan historian R. Bruce Shepard suggests that the much-revered virtue of Canadian tolerance has been mostly a sham. He does his best to disclose the sham in *Deemed Unsuitable*.

This concise account tells of the hundreds of blacks from Oklahoma who attempted to build new lives for themselves on the Canadian prairies in the early decades of this century. As a white academic, Shepard feels the need to justify his foray into what many consider "black issues." But Shepard insists that white racism constitutes a perfectly legitimate course of study for a white man interested in exploring the racism that comprises part of his heritage. Indeed, where most similar discussions focus on black experience as an anomaly, Shepard writes of pervasive, durable white racism as the social pathology.

His chronicle begins in the years following manumission, when Southern whites stepped up their campaign of brutality against African-Americans. Thousands of newly freed blacks, desperate to flee, headed to the new Indian territory, the area that would soon become the state of Oklahoma. Unfortunately, a simultaneous influx of white settlers meant that blacks ended up facing the same violence and restrictions they had hoped to leave behind in the South. Shepard's chronicle offers a rare and excellent analysis of the three-way tensions between the region's native, black and white settlers. When Oklahoma's white politicians adopted a nefarious piece of legislation that left blacks virtually disenfranchised, many African-American families looked north to the Canadian plains.

Blacks made up only a small portion (1,000 to 1,500) of the total number of Americans who migrated to Canada in the early twentieth century. White Canadians proved less confrontational and more law abiding than their American counterparts, yet they expressed the same revulsion at the idea of co-existing with black people. Shepard documents many specific instances of Canadian racism, but it is his careful discussion of the Laurier government's measures to halt black immigration that truly surprises. Shepard illustrates the way racism engendered political, social and moral corruption.

Though Shepard does not always provide enough information to support each point, he proves that Canada possessed its own virulent strain of racism. *Deemed Unsuitable* allows for a more realistic appraisal of Canada's "glorious abolitionist past." [*Quill & Quire*, 1996]

The Heart Does Not Bend

By Makeda Silvera
Random House, 272 pages

Everybody seems to be talking about whether or not it's acceptable for black people to use the "N-word." I'm not convinced it's such a terrible thing.

Why? Because "nigger" happens to be a word that black people have managed to wrench control of; a word that black men, of mostly a particular class, are using to succinctly remind each other of their shared experience and their support for one another. By using the N-word publicly they are informing everyone around them that they believe racism still exists, they are conveying what their fathers conveyed in the 1970s with raised fists, which was a gesture that many people were not too fond of at the time.

The current usage of the N-word is an example of how black people can take a hostile language and adapt it to their purpose. This is of course what most black writers struggle to do. English militates against the kind of stories many black people would like to tell. Playwright Djanet Sears concurred when I interviewed her in 1997 about her play *Harlem Duet*: "It's difficult finding the words to describe the play's racial themes," I said. "I understand," she answered: "The words just aren't out there."

Sears is a black Canadian artist gifted at finding the words. Thankfully, she's not the only one. Toronto writer Makeda Silvera has just published a novel of delicate eloquence that is a testament to her ability to make a stubborn language meet her needs.

Silvera is the author of two story collections and two anthologies featuring women of colour. *The Heart Does Not Bend*, her first novel, tells the story of Maria Galloway, the matriarch of a working-class Jamaican family. The novel is narrated by Maria's granddaughter Molly and spans the thirty-odd years from Molly's birth in 1957 to Maria's death.

The first half unfolds in Jamaica where Maria and Molly live in a comfortable home encircled by a loving family and generous friends: There are the grandaunts—flamboyant Joyce and pious Ruth—and the cultured Uncle Mikey. And there is Mammy, Maria's mother who keeps alive her grandmother's stories of slavery.

Maria has worked hard to raise four children, who remain grateful and devoted. But Maria is never really content. Her life is filled with love she makes too little of and disappointments she makes too much of. When Maria leaves Jamaica for Canada it is because she is outraged by Mikey's homosexual lifestyle, but also because she misses her three other children who have settled in Toronto.

Unfortunately, Maria's imperious behaviour, her reliance on alcohol and her intolerance of Molly's lesbian relationship—she learns nothing from her alienation of Mikey—are just a few of the issues which strain family ties.

Silvera does several things that impress when it comes to language: She refrains from exaggerating Jamaican speech in a way that might make certain figures clownish. Her dialogue is pure patois, delightfully expressive, but democratically measured. In contrast, Molly narrates in a low-key standard English that communicates her sensitive, sensual nature, but keeps her perspective from imposing.

Silvera does not allow her prose to be straightjacketed into the narrow box of linguistic terms reserved for the discussion of black experience. As with many black women writers, she focuses on dissension within the group instead of interracial strife. It's a while before we realize that this portrait of a family is also a poignant saga of Jamaican society.

In Maria, Silvera has created a completely idiosyncratic figure, strong and weak, generous and intolerant, the novel's unbending heart. Yet Maria is a type found in the work of many Caribbean-born authors: previous incarnations include Jamaica Kincaid's toxic real-life mother in her memoir *My Brother*; the mean-spirited Trinidadian grandmother in Andre Alexis' *Childhood* and Pedro's wickedly insecure mother in H. Nigel Thomas's *Behind the Face of Winter*.

What does the prominence of this figure represent in the collective Caribbean imagination? The unhappy separation of mother and child so common in the West Indies. In the novel, Maria leaves her babies with her mother while she works to purchase a home. She ends up raising her own granddaughter, Molly, and later, raises Molly's child, as well as another grandchild, Vittorio. With no fathers to speak of—this is a culture rife with invisible men—successive generations of Galloways suffer the temporary loss of both parents. These lifelong rifts compose a ruptured family narrative that staggers all the way back to slavery. Ultimately, the estrangement of mother and child symbolizes the West Indian's alienation from Africa.

Through Maria and her children, Silvera discreetly investigates questionable attitudes prevalent in Jamaican society, where sons are often favoured over daughters, fair skin favoured over dark, foreign favoured over home, and the present favoured over the past. At one point, Maria's children demand she sell her aging Kingston home. But she vociferously disagrees:

"Is forget, unna forget so quick? Is amnesia unna come down wid? Freddie, you don't remember de dead-end street? De parties, yuh kite-flying days, crab season? Peppie, yuh don't remember dat is de very yard yuh learn to fix yuh first car? Yuh forget dat when we get de house, it was just land, nothing never built on it?..."

My grandmother laughed bitterly, and now she did spit in her handkerchief. "Nobody wants to remember where dem come from..."

The Galloways' disregard for history may be the reason generation after generation continues to make the same mistakes; a gentle indictment, perhaps, of a people Silvera adores. [*Toronto Star*, 2002]

Behind the Face
of Winter
by H. Nigel Thomas
TSAR Publications, 264 pages

H. Nigel Thomas' coming-of-age novel about a West Indian teenager who settles in Montreal, *Behind the Face of Winter*, may be the starkest, most distressingly honest account of the Caribbean-Canadian experience yet written. With it, Thomas asserts his position in a tradition established by Austin Clarke, re-examined by Cecil Foster, and launched into the future by fantasy writer Nalo Hopkinson. Clarke, Foster and Hopkinson are Toronto-based English writers, whereas Thomas gives us the less explored view from Montreal—home, since the 1960s and '70s to thousands of Caribbean immigrants. That *Behind the Face of Winter* is uneven and sometimes overwritten hardly merits mention. Memories of these flaws fade like the plot of a nightmare that leaves us queasy with fear.

Appropriately, the book opens in Montreal with our hero, Pedro Moore, waking from a nightmare. It is his 26th birthday and Pedro, who is still mourning the recent death of his mother, uses the occasion to revisit the formative events of his life. He wanders back more than two decades to his childhood on the Caribbean island of Isabella where he lived with his maternal grandmother before joining his mother in Montreal.

Thomas maps out Pedro's early life at a leisurely island pace. These early passages read more like a series of interwoven sketches than a plot-driven novel. We are bewitched nonetheless. We are introduced to Pedro's grandmother Ma Moore, who is left practically destitute after her daughter departs for Canada. She soon finds a job laundering the clothes of a wealthy white man. He had taken the job away from another struggling woman in order that Ma Moore might have it: "Poor people always have for fight one another for the bones white people don't want," she tells Pedro.

Pedro's unvarying routine consists of school, where he receives a largely irrelevant colonial education, and church, where he accompanies his grandmother on Sundays. His peers consider him bookish and inconsequential. Pedro spends his free time with Sam who dispenses bawdy, fatherly advice, and the amorous Mrs. Duncan who reminds him that religion can make him sour. His island world teems with curious people and places: Mrs. Manley a rumoured *soucouyant* (vampire), the country plantation where his relatives work and the shiftless men who—like his mysterious, absent father—sow babies all over the island.

Pedro especially takes pleasure in the traditional storytellers who trade African tales featuring Doum-Doum and Anansi. Thomas, who was born in St. Vincent, possesses a spectacular ear for the music of West Indian dialect; the Doum-Doum stories and even ordinary conversations dance off the page.

The Isabella island Thomas evokes links Africa, the Old South and British colonialism with the contemporary racism Pedro meets in Canada. They are all of a piece, Thomas suggests, part of a historical continuum. Thomas writes with such fierce integrity, that we cannot doubt his bleak portrayal of the Montreal Pedro encounters in the mid-1970s. The nervous 14-year-old finds in the mother he hardly knows a vicious, unyielding, obsessively religious woman, terrified of black people and white people and the world she inhabits. At school hoodlums lurk and equally bullying administrators taunt his intelligence and anticipate failure. Alienated black children are everywhere. Pedro's new friends camouflage their despair with swaggering sexual bravado, linguistic prowess and vulgar, anti-social behaviour.

I do wish that every character in the second half of the book was delineated with as much care as Pedro and Ma Moore; what we wind up with instead is a large school portrait. Still, Thomas conveys what counts: this may be Montreal and these youngsters may be West Indian, but their lives are hardly distinguishable from blacks in the American ghetto. Indeed, Pedro's violently racist clash with Montreal police replays the harshest accounts of brutality from south of the border.

Before Thomas is accosted by the "positive police"—those who desire, on one hand, only "positive" portrayals of black Canadians, or those who insist, on the other hand, that disenfranchised blacks are "positively" figments of racist imaginations—it's important to point out that he is chronicling only a segment of the black Canadian population. Still, it is a significant segment, and one too often overlooked by contemporary black writers. In Thomas, struggling Caribbean immigrants have found a brave and eloquent voice. [*The Gazette*, 2002]

The Way Forward
Is With a Broken Heart
by Alice Walker
Random House, 200 pages

In generations to come Alice Walker will be remembered as one of a handful of authors that altered the course of American fiction. Not only for her Pulitzer Prize winning novel, *The Color Purple* (1982), in which the racially and sexually oppressed Celie survives a brutal existence by writing letters to God; but also for her groundbreaking essay *In Search of Our Mother's Gardens* (1984) that described how southern black women, released into the penury of post-slavery, rescued their sanity through artistic expression. Perhaps Walker's greatest legacy will be her recovery of the life of Harlem Renaissance writer Zora Neale Hurston—whose novel *Their Eyes Were Watching God* (1937) became the foundation for a tradition of African-American women writers.

Walker has been prolific this past decade, as an essayist, and as an outspoken environmentalist, though her output has oftened seemed less inspired. Happily, her latest book, *The Way Forward Is With A Broken Heart*, unveils a collection of simple, beautiful, sincere tales; stories about African-American women for whom change is the only constant. Described as part autobiography, part fiction, Walker's stories probe relationships between men and women, parents and children, siblings, and most thoughtfully, between blacks and whites.

The Color Purple introduced readers to a spectacularly vivid black vernacular, a sparkling language that provided Walker's southern protagonist with an authentic voice. In *The Way Forward* African-American dialect surfaces only subtly, partly because it is inappropriate to the main characters, an educated, upperwardly mobile class of women who live and work in the wider society. In the end the strong emphasis on standard English works to pull these stories squarely into the mainstream, which, of course, is exactly where they belong.

Walker composes her scenes with spare, apt detail, as in this description of the house the narrator revisits in the story "To My Young Husband":

> Its gate is the only thing left of the wooden fence we put up. The
> sweet gum tree that dominated the backyard and turned to red

and gold in autumn is dying. It is little more than a trunk. The yard itself, which I've thought of all these years as big, is tiny.

...The carport is miniscule. I wonder if you remember the steaks we used to grill there in summer, because the house was too hot for cooking, and the chilled Lambrusco we bought by the case to drink each night with dinner.

The story is based upon Walker's early marriage to a Jewish lawyer in the mid-1960s. The couple was fiercely united in their opposition to racial oppression. These were the volatile years of the civil rights movement, but Walker presents the pair as living in a bubble, their youthful optimism making them vulnerable and invulnerable the same time.

You can never tell where Walker's stories are headed. "Uncle Loaf and Auntie Putt-Putt," for example, begins with two sisters recalling their grandmother's harrowing childhood as the slave of a man who raped her regularly. But the story actually contrasts the sisters' feelings about family history and concludes with the renewal of their bond. Walker's stories present the flipside to the enduring romance of the antebellum South. The aging Auntie Putt-Putt, for instance, is a mirror image to a character like Aunt Pitty-Patt in Margaret Mitchell's *Gone With the Wind*.

Walker's stories often seem to begin at the end, hence the significance of the title: *The Way Forward Is With A Broken Heart*. In "To My Young Husband," "Orelia and John" and "Conscious Birth" marriages break down, but this only provides opportunities for new relationships to begin. Walker sees a person's sexuality as constantly evolving; a few of her divorced heroines begin romances with women.

In "Blaze," one of her bravest and most introspective pieces, characters examine their complex, uneasy friendships with white women. It's a topic that, for a number of white women, has become more taboo than interracial sex. Yet Walker navigates this emotional minefield with frankness, humour, affection and sensitivity.

A few stories in this collection have moments when they threaten to careen off course. This occurs wherever Walker gives in to her impulse to expound. Mostly though, these oddly tender evocations of life elevate the spirit. [*National Post*, 2000]

Coda

Pig Tails 'n Breadfruit

Not long ago I attended a reading at Burke's Books on St. Clair Avenue West in Toronto. The theme of the reading was Caribbean food and Sam and Rita Burke, gracious as always, had prepared a delicious spread. While the aroma of codfish, breadfruit and black pudding swirled about us, the Grenadian poet Hudson George recited from his collection, *Oil Down*. Later, Norma De Haarte regaled the audience with her tale, *Mr. Jimmy, The Black Pudding Man* and Ovid Abrams of Guyana shared tidbits from *Metegee: The History and Culture of Guyana*.

The Bajan-born author Austin Clarke was on hand as well. He read first from his popular history of slave food, *Pig Tails 'n Breadfruit*. The passage he chose tells of a village woman who is about to butcher her pig and who enterprisingly takes orders for more pounds of pork than she has pig to sell. There were snickers from the audience and nods of recognition. Next he narrated a story about a wife determined to transform her husband into a satisfying romantic partner. By then Clarke, who could barely contain his own mirth, had his listeners roaring with laughter.

Sam and Rita had set the table buffet-style and during intermission we helped ourselves to a plate. Afterward, we washed the food down with mauby and sorrel. The joy was tangible and it might even be said that the women looked the happiest, so thrilled were they to hear themselves depicted with such grace and obvious affection. That night at Burke's, it was impossible not to fall in love with Caribbean culture, and if you were of Caribbean extraction you could not help but feel a little in love with yourself.

This month I begin a column that I hope will be a place for us to enjoy our own stories from our own perspectives: for although black literature is respected internationally it is rare that the opinions of black readers make their way into the discussion. In books, as in music and film, it is primarily white critics who define black culture. We have lost control of the conversation.

When I first began reviewing books seven or eight years ago I was warned that editors might put me in a box. It was a legitimate concern, I suppose, but I *wanted* to write about artists of African ancestry. It's one of the things I thought a black critic should do. Besides, I thought I knew a secret. Many black Canadian writers, along with filmmakers and playwrights, were producing superior works. It was no secret, however. Black artists were simply not receiving their share of attention. I set out to help heighten their profiles.

These days it is more and more difficult for a black critic to find work writing about black culture. As soon as a black writer is accepted by the cultural establishment, the mainstream works hard to de-emphasize the significance of race. This may sound like a good thing, but it means that the issue of race as it appears in the work of the writer (and as it appears in the lives of black people), is hardly dealt with, or it is only handled in a way that allows white people to feel at ease. Heaven forbid a black critic should come along and discuss racism outright, even when it happens to be the subject of the book or film.

Consequently, black readers wind up distancing themselves from their own cultural figures. When an Austin Clarke or Djanet Sears or Jamaica Kincaid or George Elliott Clarke starts winning kudos from mainstream readers, we let them go. Sometimes we even push them away. And while it is right and wonderful that these authors attract such diverse audiences, it is equally important that we continue to embrace our own men and women of letters, for they are the ones who sustain us. It is through the storyteller that we come to know and love ourselves. [*Pride*, 1999]